Bust Your BUTS

Tips for Teens Who Procrastinate

Joanne Foster, Ed.D.

"Only you can control your future."
~ Dr. Seuss

Great Potential Press, Inc.
www.greatpotentialpress.com

Bust Your BUTS: Tips for Teens Who Procrastinate

Cover design: Hutchison-Frey
Interior design: The Printed Page
Edited by: Kama Cannon

Published by Great Potential Press, Inc.
1650 N. Kolb, Suite 200
Tucson, AZ 85715

Library of Congress Cataloging-in-Publication Data

ISBN 10: 978-1-935067-33-7
ISBN 13: 978-1-935067-33-8

For Cara, Allie, and Jake.
Let curiosity, knowledge, creativity, effort,
and kindness empower you.

Acknowledgments

There are several people I'd like to thank for helping me see this book through to completion expeditiously. I'm indebted to all of them for not procrastinating!

Firstly, I appreciate the sustained effort put forth by everyone at Great Potential Press. In particular, I want to acknowledge the indefatigable Dr. James T. Webb who demonstrates leadership, guidance, and foresight, and does so with affability and a smile. Janet Gore, Kama Cannon, Asa Bush, Terry Filipowicz, Julee Hutchison, and Lisa Liddy comprise an efficient, highly competent team whose hard work and dedication are unparalleled. As such, collaborating on *Bust Your BUTS* has been pleasant, productive, and invigorating! Thank you. The final product reflects your perseverance and expertise.

I am fortunate to have had four advance readers who provided me with thoughtful, valuable feedback. Dona Matthews is a friend and colleague who cheerfully offers support, knowledge, and encouragement whenever I embark upon a writing project or tackle an initiative. Craig Phillips is enthusiastic about learning, and he shares his acquired teaching expertise with every constructive suggestion. He is, indeed, a gentleman and a scholar. Barb Wiseberg has an endless supply of energy and creative ideas. She is unfailingly gracious and industrious, and makes hard work look easy. Nicki Weinberg is very astute, and has an incredible eye for detail. She's a whiz when it comes to spotting improper punctuation, spelling glitches, or grammatical inaccuracies. Thank you, Dona, Craig,

Barb, and Nicki for reading early drafts of *Bust Your BUTS*, and for sharing your perspectives and acumen.

Procrastination can be challenging, and productivity can be elusive. Many parents, teens, teachers, and other professionals willingly tell me about their concerns and experiences. They enrich my knowledge base, and I am a better and more informed writer as a result. I also recognize the positive influence that Beverley Slopen has had on me over the past several years. She consistently gives excellent advice, including insisting that I keep my writing focused and authentically relevant.

My friends continue to be a strong and steady presence in my life. With patience and good humor, they bear with me when I become immersed in my work, and they bolster my confidence. I'm appreciative that my friends are so caring and supportive.

My family conveys unconditional faith in my writing and other endeavors, and I know that I can count on them for anything. Thank you, Eric, Cheryl, Michele, and Aaron for cheering me on, and for encouraging your sweet children to do likewise. I adore you all.

I cannot even begin to express how fortunate I am that Garry Foster is by my side for every adventure, challenge, and opportunity that life brings our way. He inspires me, and makes me happy. He is enterprising, kind, smart, accomplished, and generous. Moreover, he encourages me to keep up, and to strive to be the best I can be—and I am extremely grateful for that. Thank you, Garry. This book would not have been possible without your unwavering love and support.

—Joanne
July 9th, 2017

Bust Your BUTS...

(Whose BUTS...?)

This book is for kids
To keep on their shelves
But...
Adults who read it
Just might see themselves!

Procrastination
Occurs at all ages
But...
If you want strategies,
Check out these pages.

Read this together
Or have a quick look
But...
Don't "put off" using
The tips in this book!

Author's Note: *Bust Your BUTS* is a resource that works well on its own—but...It also complements *Not Now, Maybe Later,* another book by Joanne Foster that was written for parents of procrastinators. Like jeans and a tee shirt, these two books go together. And, both contain lots of practical ideas.

Table of Contents

Introduction

This book is for TEENS!

Here's why...And, here's how to use this book to your advantage

You picked up this book because for some reason it interested you. (Or maybe someone else convinced you to have a look at it.) You may have procrastinated in getting to this page, but here you are—which means you're already on the way to busting your BUTS—also known as avoidance tendencies. Bravo!

Now what?

The first thing you should know is that reading this book will help you to help yourself. All the points are straightforward, and they relate to the BUTS that people use as reasons for procrastinating. I wrote this book to inform and inspire procrastinators. I don't lecture, criticize, ramble on endlessly, "dumb-down" material, or judge anybody in the process.

I simply believe that you can take control of your actions and attitudes, and you can choose if you want to change them. You can learn to understand your feelings, and improve your skills. You can even alter your circumstances. You can do all these things, and more. And yes, the word *you* appears in this paragraph a lot—because at the end of the day *you* are responsible for what happens in your life, including what gets done, and what doesn't get done.

However, the second thing you should know is that everybody procrastinates. There are plenty of legitimate reasons why (and we'll get to that later) but the truth is that many people put things off. Okay, so some people put things off more often than others—but I'm sure they have their reasons. In fact, because procrastination is so widespread, I wrote *Not Now, Maybe Later* (for parents of kids who procrastinate), and also *Bust Your BUTS* so kids and young adults can take ownership of their procrastination, and actually do something about it themselves.

I offer hundreds of tips within these pages. And, they work. That's because I consulted professionals (doctors, educators, researchers, and psychologists), and I also gathered loads of information based on the real-life experiences of children, teens, parents, teachers, and countless others. I collected interesting quotes, too. I pulled all of that material together, and concentrated on the most important pieces. Then, and only then, I wrote this very focused book—for procrastinators like you. And, if friends, teachers, parents, or others read it, I suspect they'll learn something, too. I hope you'll share this book with them. As I mentioned before, everybody procrastinates.

The third thing you should know is that I've organized *Bust Your BUTS* sensibly to make it easier for you to figure out the reasons why you procrastinate, and then to take practical steps to manage the procrastination. You can jump around the different sections of the book, or you can also go page-by-page-by-page from the beginning to the end, but you don't have to do that unless you want to.

I offer ideas to help you prevent and eliminate procrastination because it can be problematic. For example, procrastination can cause a substantial amount of unhappiness, stress, conflict, and even exasperation. It can affect your achievement at school or on a job, short-circuit your hopes and dreams, interfere with your relationships with other people, and compromise your productivity.

On the other hand, there may also be a plus side to procrastinating. It can allow you more time to plan things out carefully and to pay attention to detail. Perhaps you see procrastinating as a means to an end—so you can acquire resources, or spend quality time with family and friends, or do something you really enjoy doing. In fact, many people see procrastination as a kind of door leading to greater creativity; an opportunity to think, and let ideas bubble along. Depending on how you view it, there is a potential upside, as well as a downside to procrastination.

If you look at the Table of Contents, you will see many different reasons why people procrastinate. Think about which ones might apply to you. When you flip to those pages, you will get a sense of what underlies the reasons, and then you can poke through the specific suggestions for dealing with your own procrastination. Consider which tips you might like to try right away, and which ones you might want to (ahem) put off till later...

Take it one step at a time. You already took the first one when you chose to open the introductory pages of this book!

Joanne Foster, Ed.D.

2017

"The man who removes a mountain begins by carrying away small stones."

~ William Faulkner (author)

CHAPTER 1

About Procrastination

"You can't be that kid standing at the top of the waterslide, overthinking it.

You have to go down the chute."

~ Tina Fey (author, actor, comedian)

What is procrastination?

Procrastination involves putting things off. It's intentional. In other words, it's something that someone does willfully or on purpose, for a reason. And, there are *many* possible reasons (as you can see from the Table of Contents).

How do procrastinators procrastinate? Some may be slow to start a task, or they may be reluctant to finish it. Others may put things off in certain areas of their life, but be quick to do everything else. People may procrastinate at certain times of day, or year, or when they're hungry, tired, angry, or sad. They may procrastinate in a waterpark (as in the quote above), or in the kitchen, gym, or classroom. Sometimes they may be able to say why they're procrastinating, but they may also have difficulty figuring it out or explaining it. Procrastinators may think that their behavior doesn't really have an impact on anybody else, or they may realize that their procrastination does affect others but they aren't sure what to do about it.

So many factors and implications to consider!

Many people think procrastinators are lazy and disrespectful. And some are. For example, let's say you're part of a group working on a school project. If you don't do your part when you're supposed to, and your group misses the due date, then that could cause others to think you're lazy or you're disrespectful of their needs and feelings. However, if you don't do your part because of health issues, or because you're confused, or because you don't have the necessary materials, then laziness and disrespect may have nothing to do with it. It's easy for people to jump to conclusions about procrastinators, but the truth is that everyone is different, and so are the reasons for their behaviors and attitudes.

Just so you know, procrastination comes from the Latin word "procrastinare." *Pro* has to do with forward motion. *Crastinus* has to do with tomorrow. When these two word segments are placed together, the meaning has to do with putting things forward until another day. But…let's get real. Sometimes people don't get things started, and the result is that they don't get it done at all, let alone tomorrow. Does that sound familiar?

Sometimes procrastinators find something else to do instead, and in their heads they're thinking, "*I'm doing something! So, I'm not really procrastinating.*" But…they are. Substituting one activity for another means that one is being postponed till tomorrow, or maybe the day after that.

Being able to plan, start, and ultimately finish a task may involve a lot of steps. But…it's a process. And, this process can easily become derailed at any point along the way—at the beginning, middle, or end. That's because people's daily lives have become increasingly hectic.

Procrastination can happen repeatedly, and for long or short intervals, depending on the reasons for it. There are many influences out there, too, such as people or things that sway or convince us to behave in ways we might not otherwise consider. Plus, there are distractions ranging from food to fun that tempt us to procrastinate. Moreover, we experience different feelings over the course of time, and these can also affect how or whether we put things off.

Clearly, procrastination is complex, and that's why it's not just a matter of saying, "*I'm going to stop procrastinating!*" and then you will, and that'll be the end of it. It's not that simple. Certainly, procrastinators need to decide to change and to have encouragement, but they also need good strategies, and an understanding of what's causing their procrastination in the first place. Procrastinators also have to get past the guilt of procrastinating so they can focus instead on how to become more productive. They may need help developing a *forward motion* plan that has a greater emphasis on *now* rather than on *tomorrow*—or the tomorrows after that.

Is procrastination bad and are there ways around it, or are you forever doomed?

> *"Failures, repeated failures, are finger posts on the road to achievement.*
>
> *One fails forward toward success."*
>
> ~ C. S. Lewis (author)

The word "doomed" implies hopelessness, or being destined for failure. Let's look at the likelihood of that in relation to putting things off. Say you don't do your homework. You decide to avoid it, and you have no specific plan as to when you might get to it. Maybe in the next day or two. Maybe not. What will the consequences be? Truthfully, you may end up not learning what you should; you'll disappoint your parents and teachers; you'll be letting down your classmates; and you probably won't be able to progress as readily to the next level in your schoolwork. That's all pretty important stuff.

However, the sun will come up, you will still be able to function, and you may even learn from the experience. Moreover, you may have a *very good reason* for not doing your homework. For example, it may be too easy, or too hard, or not relevant. Or you may be too busy, or tired, or distracted. Regardless, you are NOT doomed.

If people don't do their laundry, they don't have clean clothes. If they don't put on their shoes, they go barefoot. If they don't brush their teeth, they get cavities. There are consequences for everything we choose to do or not to do. Some consequences are far more serious than others, especially if they involve health or safety concerns. The key is to think about why you aren't doing something, and also what might happen as a result of not doing it. If you procrastinate, are you willing to live with what happens as a result? Will it have an impact on anyone else? Is there some way to start slowly, or to work with others, or to find a way around whatever it is that's causing you to put the task off?

There's always something you can do. And, you don't have to do it alone. Enlist help. Look for alternatives. Get creative. Read the ideas throughout this book. You are NOT doomed!

Procrastination and power struggles? (And at what cost?)

> *"Whenever you're in conflict with someone, there is one factor that can make the difference between damaging your relationship and deepening it.*
>
> *That factor is attitude."*
>
> ~ William James (philosopher)

Sometimes procrastination arises because of a power struggle, such as when teens don't or won't do something that their parents or other adults want them to do. For example, say you've been asked to clean your room and you keep procrastinating. Before long, you and your parents are at a standoff, and everyone is upset.

The real question to consider here is not *how to win* these types of conflicts, but *how to prevent* them, because there really isn't a win-win scenario once a power struggle gets underway. It's uncomfortable, tense, unproductive, and people can end up saying things they later regret. These kinds of situations are best avoided altogether.

So, instead of wondering, *"How can I win this power struggle?"* try to think more constructively. Ask yourself, *"How can I avoid this conflict?"* Here are five steps to try. They all start with the letter C so they'll be easy to remember, and, to share with your parents who can use them, too.

Steps for avoiding conflict:

1. **Calm down**—Pause and collect your thoughts. Take stock of what's what, including people's feelings, and the potential consequences of your actions, before getting yourself (and possibly others) into a snit.

2. **Communicate**—Listen. Chat. Share ideas. Be open to having a discussion rather than a quarrel about whatever is causing the problem. Use a steady tone of voice, not an argumentative or blameful one. If you're not sure what to say, you can also remain silent. Silence can speak volumes.

3. **Cooperate**—Think about how to work alongside someone else, to find a way to overcome the conflict. Don't be afraid to ask questions in order to learn how to resolve things as a team.

4. **Compromise**—Show a willingness to be flexible, to be fair, and to meet other people halfway. Be respectful of their viewpoints even though they may differ from your own.

5. **Consider**—Consider an action plan. Then once you've agreed on a way forward, demonstrate that you're capable, confident, and able to see things through.

Put all of these suggestions together, and you will have a powerful strategy for dealing with procrastination-related disagreements, rather than getting caught up in a power struggle. In the whole scheme of things, that will be far more productive!

However, if a power struggle is already in the works, here is a useful tip to help de-escalate it. Give yourself some space and time to re-set your thinking and behaviors. Taking a little time apart from one another gives people a chance to reflect, deal with their feelings, consider other people's perspectives, and calm down. (There's that first C word again. It's really important.)

Remember, we don't always agree with others. Disagreements are part of life. Nevertheless, it is seldom helpful for us to use procrastination to express our anger at others or even to assert our independence, and we can work toward not being defiant, angry, overwhelmed, or disrespectful. We can think about whether a confrontation is necessary, if it's worth the hassle, and whether the problem or challenge might even subside on its own. Stepping back from the "battle field" allows us to do that. Compromising, or giving in a bit, is also an option. (For instance, picking up your dirty clothes and wet towels from the floor won't make your room *clean*, but it might serve as a peace-making move. You could show your parents you're willing to at least start the process, helping to avoid further conflict.) Sometimes the solution to a challenging situation turns out to be easier than you might have anticipated.

In the chapters that follow, you will see hundreds of strategies to overcome procrastination, and many of them are possible solutions that can affect whether or not conflicts or power struggles will arise. You will also find ways to be productive. The bottom line, however, is that *you* will have to be involved and take responsibility for your actions—or inaction. As Benjamin Franklin said, *"Tell me and I forget. Teach me and I remember. Involve me and I learn."* In the spirit of those words, I invite you to continue reading, to get involved in dealing with your procrastination, and to see how you can become more purposeful and overcome it.

CHAPTER 2

Personal Reasons for Procrastination: What Are Your BUTS?

"Begin at the beginning and go on till you come to the end; then stop."

~ Lewis Carroll (author)

BUT...I have too much to do

Life is crammed with demands. That means there's often pressure to get things done. You probably have several school assignments, and perhaps you promised to help wash the dishes, or clean the garage, and water the plants, too. People are expecting you to see things through. Deadlines are looming; too much, too soon. There simply isn't enough time to do everything! And, you're feeling overwhelmed. So, you're procrastinating. It's a way of coping with the many demands.

When you look at the combined size of those tasks, perhaps you automatically think, "*This is massive!*" and procrastinate. It's almost as if you're jamming on the brakes. However, when that happens, you might as well be sitting in one place with your wheels spinning, going nowhere.

Fortunately, you can adjust your way of thinking. You can set a workable pace without having to go into brake mode. This means making wise choices about how you approach the problems or demands. No one is born knowing how to make good decisions about time management or pacing. And when confronted with piles of demands (real or imagined), it helps to take a step back and think about what's involved. If you would like to learn more about making decisions, check out Beatrice Elyé's book, *Teen Success! Ideas to Move Your Mind.*[1]

It might also be helpful to see any compilation of demands as a kind of "folder" of several things to do, not as one enormous undertaking. You don't have to program yourself toward completing everything at once. You can make a conscious decision to focus on one task at a time. So, instead of pressing the brakes you're going forward—slowly, steadily, and comfortably.

A framework for positive action starts by getting calm, and feeling that you *can* do what you have to do. Emotions like worry and guilt influence how you'll react to requests, suggestions, or expectations, and emotions have a direct bearing on whether you'll be motivated. If you feel overwhelmed, it's important to try and get rid of that feeling. For example, you could start with thinking about how to cope with the amount of stuff that's piling up by putting a priority on different parts of it, and then figuring out the amount of time, energy, and willpower you'll likely need to tackle it. Or at least some of it!

Here are some realistic tips to help you overcome procrastination and manage demands when you feel overwhelmed.

. . . .

TIPS for when you procrastinate because you have too much to do

○ **Get specific.** What exactly has to be done, and why? Know what's required of you. Make a to-do list. It may not be as long or as complicated as you think.

○ **Can you cluster some things together?** If you can put things into the same "bucket," then you will have fewer buckets to manage. Maybe you can combine "like tasks," such as gathering resource material for several assignments in one fell swoop, instead of spreading the research demands over time.

○ **When are the deadlines?** When does each thing on the draft list have to be completed? Mark it down. Find out if there's any flexibility.

○ **Prioritize.** Based on the timelines you've determined, put the tasks in order. Your list of priorities might be based on what you feel is *most urgent*. (What has to be done immediately?) Or your priorities might be based on what's really *most important*. (What matters the most to you—or others—today?) Or your priorities might also be based on the *long term*. (What's going to matter a great deal in the future?) For more on priorities, see the third section in Chapter 3 of this book.

○ **Number everything.** It will simplify things. You'll want to be able to refer back to your list of priorities. You may even want to shift the priorities around once you begin working through them.

○ **Break it down and "chunk" it.** Divide the first task into manageable chunks. Focus on that one portion for now. Try not to get sidetracked by the other items on your list.

○ **Are you ready?** Gather together any materials or equipment you think you will need for that one task so you'll be ready to begin. Stay true to your intent. That is, don't start rearranging your playlist, or poking through a pile of stuff you own, or allow yourself to get involved in some other activity that's non-productive.

○ **Take that one crucial step.** Just one. This will start you moving forward. It will also help you begin to appreciate the pleasures of the path once you've begun. There's an old proverb, *"Every great journey starts with one small step."*

○ **Woohoo!** Congratulate yourself on that step, and then take another...

○ **Give yourself a break.** As you proceed, take time out. It may be a walk, a snack, or a visit with friends—whatever you like—and don't feel guilty about it. But remember, there's a difference between a short break, a vacation, and an escape.

○ **Get help if you need it.** Ask for assistance or direction if you get bogged down. Sometimes people confront obstacles or stumble when trying to advance. It's okay to ask for help, and it can even be a more efficient approach to getting things done.

○ **Imagine the results.** Tell yourself, *"I can do this, and I can do it well."* (But it doesn't have to be perfect!)

○ **Pace yourself.** What if partway through the task you find that you have to focus your attention on something that's more urgent? What if another important responsibility comes along? You can *temporarily* veer off course. If you do, follow the same process listed above. Start by breaking down that task so it's easier to manage and isn't overwhelming.

○ **Check your list.** Keep up to date. Cross things off your to-do list once you've done them (hooray!), or add them as they arise.

• •

On page 14 of my previous book, *Not Now, Maybe Later,* I emphasize that procrastinators often find that whatever they're confronting is not nearly as bad or as big as they had thought. When something seems overwhelming, you might want to ask yourself, *"Is this problem a pebble, a rock, a boulder, or a mountain?"* Think of the points outlined above as a strategic plan for reducing, getting around, or scrambling over the obstacle.

Remember that keeping up with tasks and activities may involve dealing with supposedly large things (boulders), or unwieldy masses of small ones (pebbles), any of which can become discouraging. Keeping up also involves learning how to manage time effectively. Time has a way of disappearing.

Have you ever thought about how you use time during the day? Are you wasteful? Do you have sensible routines in place? Do you do things logically or randomly? It makes good sense to think about how you use (or fritter away) time, and how you can become more efficient. Then you won't feel overwhelmed, and you'll be less apt to procrastinate. (I discuss time management more fully in Chapter 3 and in Chapter 5.)

Try to be smart about what *must* get done. Many things that seem urgent actually aren't as pressing as we think, although we can fall into a trap of reacting to those that seem oh-so-important at any given moment. When there are too many demands, and only so much time, that's when life becomes overwhelming. Narrow down your to-do list—for example by eliminating nonessential tasks, or finding a shortcut or quick fix for some of them, or shifting them over to someone else. (In other words, you can remove, revamp, or reallocate.) In fact, you might decide to procrastinate on purpose because you may recognize that some things can be put off or transferred to another to-do list—for the time being. It doesn't mean you're neglectful or slacking off. You may actually be strategic! (Although if you are uncaring, then please read on…)

BUT…I don't care

Do you have a blasé attitude? Perhaps it simply doesn't matter to you whether something gets done or not. So, you procrastinate. As far as you're concerned, it'll wait. It's no big deal. You may not see any connection with your life. Or you may have better things to do. Or maybe you're thinking, "*I'll get to it eventually, and that's fine.*" Here is where decision-making skills come in handy again. Choices have consequences.

It may be fine with you to postpone things, but it may not be fine with others who might be affected by your procrastination. Say you're involved with a group project or team sports, and you decide to procrastinate. Friends or teammates could receive a poor grade or miss an opportunity because you didn't do your part. Is that fair? Sometimes you may not even realize who else might feel the impact of your attitude or behavior, immediately or over time.

If you are the only one who will reap benefits or face penalties when you decide to do something or not do it, then that's your call. If you aren't interested in a task or activity, and you have no reason to proceed, and you choose to procrastinate—then so be it. Maybe you'll care more about it in a day or two. One way to make that happen is to determine how the task might have some value to you or to others. You'll be more inclined to do something if it's meaningful to you, or to the people you encounter daily.

However, if you can't find any relevance, and you still don't care, and your procrastination turns into disregard for other people, or a lack of respect or courtesy, then that's a problem.

When you opt to suit yourself, or you wait till the time is right just for you, it's possible that you're being self-indulgent—that is, putting your own needs ahead of the needs of friends or family. If so, these people may believe you're inconsiderate.

Here are some tips to help you become more thoughtful and in tune with others.

TIPS for when you procrastinate because you just don't care

○ **Assess possible outcomes.** Think carefully—who else is likely to experience an impact from your decision to procrastinate? And, how will they feel about this? Will they be disappointed? Angry? Embarrassed? Do you care about *that?*

○ **Connect with your own feelings.** Consider how you react when people let *you* down. What message are they conveying? How does that make you feel?

○ **What matters to you?** Figure out what you do care about. Create a list, and then make connections between what's on it and what you are expected to do. For example, I have no interest in trucks. I would not want to study them, drive them, or write a book about mechanical engineering. However, I am interested in how people live, so I would be keen to interview truck drivers in order to find out what life is like on the road. Connecting my interests with something that I don't care about makes me begin to care, or at least makes the task more interesting to me.

○ **What else matters to you?** Again, figure out what you do care about, but in relation to how you get along with others. Is kindness on your list? How about courtesy? If, in the course of your procrastinating, people think that you're insensitive or that you tend to think only about your own needs or interests, you may soon find yourself on the outs. Keep in mind that people are not usually tolerated for very long if they repeatedly disrupt or compromise others' activities or learning.

○ **Participate.** Connect meaningfully with your friends and your community, and resolve to engage in some way. You might want to get involved with community service or volunteering. If so, you'll learn about open-mindedness, fairness, punctuality, self-discipline, helpfulness, and collaboration—and become more caring in general.

○ **Any inspirational thoughts?** There are tons of famous (and not so famous but terrific) quotes about caring and attitudes.[2] You might find some that provide fresh insights, and help you become more action-oriented. For example, Prince William of Britain said, "*My guiding principles are to be honest, genuine, thoughtful, and caring.*" And philosopher Lao Tzu said, "*From caring comes courage.*" Excellent words to live by.

○ **Keep going.** Once you do start, be persistent. Remember that others may be counting on you to keep up and to contribute in some way.

○ **Start with one hurdle.** Make an effort to change your perspective about just *one* thing you don't care about, and see how it goes. Share your progress and thoughts with someone so they can offer encouragement and reinforce your effort.

○ **Add a new element.** Try adding some music, movement, art, or drama to a task that you don't want to do. If it's more interesting, you might care about it more, and be less likely to procrastinate.

○ **Inject some creativity.** Creativity can fuel enthusiasm and help to solve thorny problems. When people use their imaginations, they find innovative solutions and alternative ways to approach tasks. So, instead of putting things off or avoiding tasks, you can forge new pathways and try new, exciting methods. This applies to room clean up, assignments, and dreary household chores. Be creative! (Check this endnote for five questions that will spark your creativity.)[3]

○ **Ask those you trust.** Find out how your parents and teachers go about tackling something that they aren't inclined to do. What strategies do they use to counteract a negative or uncaring attitude?

• •

Try to make it a point to start caring when it's a challenge, even if it's only a bit of caring at a time. You can make a positive difference, and accomplish more than you might imagine. Being a caring person will help you feel good about yourself, and it will strengthen your connections with others. Research studies show that virtues like kindness, learning to give and receive graciously, and empathy lead to happiness, and greater success in life. Those virtues, and others like them, contribute to strength of character—probably the greatest strength any one person can have—but you have to work at it.

BUT...I'm bored

You may be surprised to learn this, but boredom is actually a good thing! When people are bored, they have an opportunity to think about what they would like to do, what really interests them, and how they can be more productive. Boredom allows for daydreaming and wishful thinking, including how to harness and extend curiosity. Boredom is a time of recharging, and of stillness.[4] Boredom can lead to self-discovery and action!

When boredom becomes a reason for procrastinating, however, and a person says, for example, *"I don't want to do my homework because I'm bored,"* that might be a whole different story. It might be that the person prefers to do something that is more appealing at that moment. But it's also quite possible that the work is not a good "fit." In that case, boredom becomes a warning sign that things aren't quite right.

Sometimes that poor fit may be called boredom because the person isn't sure what else to say it is. The task may be too scary or too hard. Instead of admitting to it, or to being unhappy, hesitant, or frustrated, it might be easier—as in less embarrassing or more acceptable—to acquire some distance and just say, *"I'm bored!"* and leave it at that. In this situation, honesty, and perhaps better organizational and time management skills, may be in order.

More often than not though, boredom is a result of being under-challenged. For example, if work is too *easy*, it will be of little interest. (You may have already learned and mastered it.) Or it may feel *tedious, repetitive*, or *dull*. (Have you ever been asked to complete a zillion math questions that are all more or less the same? If you can prove you know the math principles after finishing a few questions, why won't that do?) Or the task may *lack relevance*. (It may appear to have nothing to do with your life; it doesn't matter to you, or it lacks a creative spark to make it motivating—like having to memorize a long list of words.) Or it may seem *silly*. (Like being told to wear or eat or do something foolish just because other people say so.)

Explanations like those—simplicity, monotony, pointlessness, and foolishness—are all potential reasons for being bored, and for procrastinating. What can you do to remedy these kinds of situations? Here are some suggestions.

· ·

TIPS for when you procrastinate because you're bored

○ **Get to the source.** What's causing you to feel bored? Zero in on the reason so you can address it. Is it too easy? Too dull?

○ **Admit it.** If saying, *"I'm bored"* is just a handy catchall phrase or a way out that you're using even though you're not actually bored, then give that some careful thought. What's really at the root of your avoidance behavior? If it truly is boredom, then try adding fun or creativity into the task—for instance, be inventive by making it a game, by role-playing, or by adding an element of physical activity. If all else fails, just take a deep breath and do what must be done quickly so you can move on to something else.

○ **Who is at fault?** So, you're bored. Whose problem is it? Yours alone? Or yours and the teacher's? Or yours and your parent's combined? Work together to set expectations that are fair. What is a fair and suitable task? Choose one that you can do in a reasonable amount of time, with some effort.

○ **Advocate for yourself.** Does your ability level match up properly with what is being asked of you? Expectations should align with what you can realistically accomplish. They should not be too simple, but not too hard either. Challenge in moderation is good. And, be forewarned that this will likely involve some work by you as part of the deal. If there is a "mismatch" between the requirements of the task, and your capability, then speak up! Respectfully, of course. There are smart steps for self-advocacy. In brief, they include getting your facts straight; working alongside others you trust; making sure you have a reachable goal and a sensible timeline; and staying focused.[5]

○ **Find a hook.** Same-old-same-old *is* boring. Is there some way to "own" or "reinvent" the task, and make it more unique or stimulating?[6] Even a *little* excitement or challenge can be motivating and help to generate enthusiasm, and that can forestall procrastination.

○ **Enthusiasm is like having your own "special power."** Think of it as a magic elixir or personally motivating force, designed to give you a purposeful boost and get rid of procrastination. Fiction is full of characters with enhanced abilities, and even "special powers."[7] Many of these characters call upon energy, knowledge, or strength in order to triumph. You may not be "powerful" in the sense that you can save the entire world, but with enthusiasm you can change your own world.

○ **Exercise.** It will invigorate you so you will feel less lethargic. Honest.

○ **Who's doing what?** Do you find that other people (such as friends or family members) end up doing stuff for you, while you end up sitting around being bored? Why is that? Think about how to push yourself to contribute more, and perhaps share the load equitably. Talk with those "other people" about this.

○ **Entertainment 24/7?** Some teens like to be entertained all the time, and don't know what to do with themselves when they find they have a lull in their activity schedule. They claim they're bored when things aren't enjoyable or entertaining, and so they procrastinate. However, not everything in life is amusing, fun, compelling, or fascinating. Try to find balance by accepting that some things are going to seize your attention and be pleasurable, whereas other demands will require that you put forth more effort if you're going to become engaged and stay on task.

○ **Use the boredom!** Resolve to do what needs to be done as fast as possible. Then, take the extra time and do something you enjoy. Or better still, if you have time on your hands, why not do something nice for others?

Give some thought as to how serious your boredom might be. If you're finding *everything* dull and dreary, you might need professional help in order to re-engage with school and other activities. If your boredom is rooted in depression, helplessness, loss, or anger there may be some deeper issues, and a family counselor or therapist may be able to assist you or offer guidance. Be sure to ask for this help. A professional perspective can provide you with important and constructive feedback, fresh insights, direction, and confidence.

BUT…I'm not confident

Self-confidence builds as we learn from experience, celebrate efforts, and develop strengths. Confidence has a lot to do with what's already happened in our lives, but it's also connected with our attitudes about the present, and toward the future.

You might not know this, but there are two widespread beliefs that are not true, and that can interfere with the development of strong self-confidence.

The first false belief is that people are either confident or insecure; either one or the other. That's not realistic. In fact, very few people (children, teens, or adults) feel really good (or really bad) about themselves in every area of life. For example, you might be confident about your ability in math, but not confident about making friends.

The second false belief is that praise makes people feel confident. A strong sense of self is built on feeling genuinely capable in areas that matter to you (whether it's creative writing, or hockey, or whatever), with emphasis on the word *genuinely*. Hollow, insincere, or overly gushy praise can lessen a person's confidence because it doesn't feel real or properly earned.

Sometimes people who lack self-confidence will procrastinate because they don't have faith in their ability to do something. As a result, they'll put it off or find ways to avoid doing it. It's important to realize that not everyone is skilled at everything. And, that's certainly the case when beginning something new. Sometimes all you need is a little encouragement, and maybe some assistance or guidance, to determine what steps to take, and how to begin.

You can learn to define your own success, and the path you want to take to get there. It may be by improving on something you can already do, or by progressing a little rather than a lot. Success is not necessarily about grades. Or prizes. Or applause. Success means something different to everyone. If you're willing to challenge your understandings of success, and you don't focus exclusively on big accomplishments, you'll experience more successes—and greater confidence. I recently saw a poster that indicated ten things that require zero talent, but that can help people succeed. (If you want to try guessing, don't peek below...)

The ten things are: being on time; work ethic; effort; body language; energy, attitude; passion; being coachable; doing extra; and being prepared. I'm not suggesting here that you or anyone else has zero talent, but I am suggesting that everyone can follow through on these actions, and gain confidence in the process.

Here are some strategies to help you become confident about taking on challenges as opposed to putting them off.

. . . .

TIPS for when you procrastinate due to a lack of self-confidence

○ **Appreciate what you can do, and do it!** Some things will come easily to you, whereas other things will be difficult and require more effort. Everyone is unique. Try not to be too self-critical. Celebrate your small steps and accomplishments as well as the bigger ones. Albert Einstein said, *"The value of achievement lies in the achieving."* Little bits add up.

○ **Find the enjoyment.** Confidence grows as we experience things we like to do, and become better at doing them. So, enjoy what you do. What interests you? Think about how you can tap into those interests when you confront a challenge and are tempted to avoid it or to procrastinate.

○ **Get a "cheerleader."** Who can you count on to offer constructive comments about your progress, to make you feel good, and to keep you motivated? This is especially helpful when you hit snags or when you have to reconsider options, review goals, or adjust your efforts to adapt to changing circumstances, deadlines, or demands.

○ **Do you get sidetracked?** If you focus on one thing at a time, it will be easier to stay confident. When you get bogged down or have too much happening at once, it can be tougher to feel confident moving forward.

○ **Develop a growth mindset.** Those who have a growth mindset believe that people develop their abilities over time by taking advantage of opportunities to learn. Instruction and guidance are also important. If you find yourself putting off a task, you might be wondering, "*Can I do this?*" or thinking, "*I can't do this.*" However, thoughts are like a framework for action. Is it a problem you are facing, or is it a challenge? People with a growth mindset think, "*I can do this.*" They look for a way forward, thrive on challenge, and actively figure out how to get past limitations. You won't know if you're able to do something until you try! (For more on growth mindsets, check out this endnote.[8])

○ **Believe in yourself.** Have hopes. Have dreams. Make them happen.[9] You'll feel confident by succeeding in areas that matter to you. And no one succeeds at everything, so if you falter don't lose faith in yourself. See it as chance to review steps, adjust your efforts, and learn. Who you are, and what you can achieve, is not predetermined. It evolves. Tennis champion Serena Williams says, "*I think losing makes me even more motivated.*"

○ **Look back.** Uncertainty can compromise your self-assurance and your initiative, and before you know it you're procrastinating. Look at your past successes, and consider what you did to be successful. How did you overcome difficulties? How did you meet challenges? Try to rekindle those sparks so you can move forward with assurance and determination.

○ **Buddy up.** If you do something with someone else, it helps give you confidence, plus you'll be preparing yourself to do it independently later. Teamwork can be motivating. And fun, too.

○ **Develop a "word cloud."** Consider creating a concept map (or word cloud) to post in your room or elsewhere, to motivate you and to help you visualize your achievements. Just go online to the word clouds site[10] and input important ideas. (The fewer the words, the more concise the cloud.) For example, I extracted lots of key concepts from these past few pages on building self-confidence, and the site generated this sample "thumbs up" shaped word cloud.

Colorful and focused designs such as this can serve to focus your attention and boost your morale when you're tempted to procrastinate. You can create your own word cloud on whatever topic moves you—as wordy, complex, or targeted as you like—and let it inspire you!

○ **Ask for help if you need it.** Get the assistance you require. You will develop confidence as you progress, and you will be more motivated to keep going and to get things done.

○ **Set realistic goals for yourself.** If you strive for goals that are attainable, you will feel self-assured and proud once you reach them. This will help you aspire to set and get started on new goals rather than procrastinate. Think about striving toward short-term outcomes before aiming for long-term ones (such as writing an introductory paragraph, not the whole essay), or small accomplishments before large ones (such as creating a draft outline before composing an entire story).

• •

Self-confidence goes hand in hand with a positive attitude. Try this: use your imagination and try "projecting" yourself through a virtual portal and into the future. The task you were procrastinating over is now done. You've completed it successfully, and you feel good about it! Imagine the relief and the pride. Positivity is energizing and confidence-building. And, even bad feelings can become good ones once you actually begin a challenge, see things through, and meet a deadline. Just give yourself whatever push you need to get to that point. You'll never get anywhere by standing still.

BUT...I might do badly (fear of failure)

Low self-confidence and lack of certainty can lead to fear. This is a reaction that people often experience when they're worried or stressed, and it can interfere with productivity and lead to procrastination. Sometimes, anxious feelings are part of a larger issue, so if you have physical distress or your fear is so intense that it affects your ability to function well or happily, it may be helpful to speak to a health care professional about your concerns.

Fear is kind of like an ocean surge that washes over someone and, like waves, it comes in different sizes, for different reasons, and at different times. It can be sudden or it can build over time. And, it can elicit different responses such as crying, anger, quivering, or hysteria. Sometimes a person will just stop right then and there when confronting fear, almost paralyzed, and not know how to cope with it or what to do next. Others try to escape from the fear by running away from it or by getting busy doing other things. Still others strive to overcome it.

What do you tend to do when something makes you fearful? You might avoid the fear-inducing situation altogether. Or you could find help, or some other means of handling it. Or, maybe you procrastinate.

When fear strikes, what people generally need is a way to feel calm and centered—to realize that they have some control over the situation in order to minimize or eliminate the fear, and to find the courage to move forward. There is no one strategy or intervention that will work equally well for all of us, or all fears, or all times, so it may be necessary to try out various possibilities in order to find the strategy that's most helpful.[11]

Perhaps you're procrastinating because of worry or stress about doing something poorly. For example, the fear that's getting you down might be a queasy or uneasy feeling about a school assignment that seems too lengthy or difficult. And, although the fear you're experiencing may not have a serious negative impact on your entire life or well-being, it *is* causing you to put off doing what you're supposed to do. In these kinds of situations, the fear-soothing suggestions that follow here might be helpful.

. . . .
TIPS for when you procrastinate because you are fearful

○ **Nip it in the bud.** The more fear builds, the more it will continue to bother you. Once you let fear grow, it gains strength and becomes harder to eliminate. Try focusing on feel-good thoughts or things you can control, such as breathing, as a way of calming down when you experience fearful or worrying situations. This takes practice but it will help you to "rewire" your thinking early and be less of a worrier.[12]

○ **It's okay to be scared.** (Or disappointed or sad or…) Learn to recognize your fears when you experience them. Name them. For example, you may be *worried* because of the length of time it will take to do a project, or *angry* because it's too complicated, or *embarrassed* because you think others might laugh if you do it incorrectly. Acknowledge the specific feeling underlying your fear and causing procrastination. Knowing what that feeling actually is will help you to understand it, and then ultimately deal with it. Accepting fear can loosen its grip, and allow you to release it.[13]

○ **Find your strengths.** Think of all your accomplishments, all the things you can do. I co-wrote an article with my friend Rina, who is an award-winning artist, and in it we discuss some challenges we experience. Do we procrastinate, or avoid painting or writing when it's difficult? No! Rina and I take a leap of faith when things seem tough, though we often have to dig down deep to find inner strength when fear seems to make it impossible to pick up a paintbrush or grapple with words. We also recognize the comfort and fear-reducing effects of home. That familiarity brings each of us a feeling of security and contentment, and it fortifies our ability to succeed. Perhaps these tips can help you.[14]

○ **Procrastination is not a way to save face.** You might be fearful of criticism or of having your task judged, and think that by procrastinating you may avoid that possibility. You might assume it's better if people believe you're late or unhurried rather than incapable. Think again. Not doing something is *not* evidence of your capability. Quite the contrary. To some people it's evidence of a default— of you copping out.

○ **Skip the fearful part—for now.** Ask yourself, is the entire task dreadful? Are there aspects of it that can be set aside, while in the meantime you begin the less frightening parts? Perhaps someone can assist you with the fear-inducing bits later. But for now, at least you will be making progress and gaining momentum.

○ **Conquering fear can take time.** You can't expect to become less fearful about something in the blink of an eye. Be prepared to work your way through the fear by using strategies such as finding supportive friends or family, reflecting on different ways to approach the task, and visualizing positive outcomes. This takes time and patience. Overcoming procrastination that is due to fear can be particularly hard because initially, when you procrastinate, the anxiety usually decreases, which feels good. Of course, later the anxiety and fear come back even stronger. But, if you procrastinate at that time, then you get a temporary lessening of anxiety once again. Can you see how it can be hard to break that vicious circle? Be patient with yourself. Be persistent, too.[15]

○ **What's the worst scenario?** What exactly are you afraid of? What might happen? Get the facts. You are bright, and you can sort it out. For example, maybe you're afraid to enroll in a dance program because you think it will be too demanding, or you'll have to perform in front of an audience and they will laugh at you. What really is the evidence for whether the worst scenario would occur? Gather all the information you need to alleviate your fears, gain confidence, and make a smart decision. Dale Carnegie (a writer and lecturer) said, *"First ask yourself: What is the worst that can happen? Then prepare to accept it. Then proceed to improve on the worst."*

○ **Gradual exposure.** Often, it's easier to conquer a fear if you take small, gradual steps. This allows you to acknowledge the fear, as well as to become comfortable and maybe even relax before you take more steps. For example, if you're afraid to ride a bicycle, or go on a boat ride, you could start by sitting for a while on the bike or in the boat without moving. You can visualize what you plan to do and how you will take the next steps. Remember, every kind of ability—even confronting fears and overcoming procrastination—grows step by step. It's also helpful if someone is there to encourage you as you take those steps.

○ **Failure as a gift?** Yes, there's an interesting best-selling book about this.[16] (And the author, Jessica Lahey, reveals that she composed many botched draft manuscripts before coming up with the final written version.) The truth is that when people learn to welcome failure, rather than fearing it or avoiding the possibility of encountering it, they open themselves to learning from their experiences and setbacks. They become more resilient in the face of obstacles and fears. So, failure is really just another one of life's learning curves. Musician Alicia Keys insists that failure is not an option for her. *"I've erased the word 'fear' from my vocabulary, and I think when you erase fear, you can't fail."*

○ **Get a dose of reality.** Just because you think you can't do something well doesn't mean you should be fearful of it. Think of the people you admire, and check out their "backstories." Chances are you'll discover that they've overcome numerous fears and failures, and that they don't excel at everything either.[17] The following words spoken by celebrated individuals from very different walks of life reflect this. (There's one for every day of the week plus a couple extra.) Perhaps these words will inspire you next time you feel inclined to procrastinate due to a fear of failure.

  ❖ Professional basketball player Michael Jordan: *"I've failed over and over and over again in my life, and that is why I succeed."*

  ❖ Musician Jon Bon Jovi: *"Success is falling down nine times and getting up ten."*

  ❖ Scientist Marie Curie: *"Nothing in life is to be feared, it is only to be understood. Now is the time to understand more, so that we may fear less."*

- ❖ Businessman Bill Gates: *"It's fine to celebrate success but it is more important to heed the lessons of failure.*

- ❖ Actress Emma Watson: *"I don't want the fear of failure to stop me from doing what I really care about."*

- ❖ Publisher Malcolm Forbes: *"Failure is success if we learn from it."*

- ❖ Nobel Prize winner, educational advocate, and teen author Malala Yousafzai: *"Don't be afraid—if you are afraid you can't move forward."*

- ❖ Poet Maya Angelou: *"Nothing will work unless you do."*

- ❖ Statesman Winston Churchill: *"Success consists of going from failure to failure without loss of enthusiasm."*

• •

Ask friends, family, and other people you know to share some of the inspiring words or stories that have helped them get on track, stay there even when it's challenging, and then go that extra distance.

Doing something when you're scared is a sign of bravery. Remember the Cowardly Lion in the Wizard of Oz? He tolerated and then overcame his fears. They didn't hold him back. Why let new or potentially scary experiences frighten you?

BUT...I might do so well that I'll be expected to do more (fear of success)

"Success is not final, failure is not fatal: it is the courage to continue that counts." It just so happens that Winston Churchill said these words, too. In a nutshell, it means that courage, and the resolve to keep going, is what helps people get to the top of their game. This involves putting forth the best possible effort.

Sometimes, however, people procrastinate because they're afraid that if they succeed, then expectations will be raised. And so, they will be asked to do even more. It's fine to extend oneself because it invites new opportunities, and it can also boost confidence. However, raised expectations might seem unfair or stifling to someone who is content to just get stuff done and out of the way. Sometimes, people are perfectly happy with what they've already accomplished, and they don't want the added pressure that can come with having to go even further than they'd expected.

So, when a parent or teacher or friend says something like, "I really like that awesome poster you drew for the school cafeteria!" and asks you to draw a few more, it can be off-putting. You created a terrific poster; however, it doesn't mean you want to draw other ones for the hallway or the gym. And that's okay. You can stand your ground respectfully. But try not to let the fear of doing too well interfere with your initiative or productivity, or you may never know what else you might have been able to do.

Before you refuse or procrastinate, consider the extent of the request, or the "add-on" to the request. For instance, what's the time commitment? Who else will be involved? How much work will you have to do? Will it interfere with other responsibilities? What is the value of the task? (That is, who is going to benefit, and what will you learn from doing it?)

When you start off strong and do something successfully, it feels great. It's also affirming when others appreciate your accomplishments. So, when expectations get "raised" as a result, you might want to ask yourself if you're ready for that challenge—and anticipate the satisfaction that will come along with it when you succeed yet again. If you're inclined to hesitate when asked to do something, consider your options and feelings. Before you choose whether to follow through, choose to think it through.

Psychologist Robert Sternberg said, *"Wisdom is knowing what choice to make."* I think success and managing expectations is also about knowing what choice to make.

Here are some ways to get past a fear of doing too well.

· ·

TIPS for when you procrastinate because you fear success

○ **Find the joy in success.** Being successful means that you've achieved something to be proud of. Success can be gratifying, motivating, and fun. Look at the upside. Resolve to yourself that there's pleasure to be had in keeping the momentum going.

○ **Stick to your limits, if that's your preference.** Be respectful and say what you're willing to do—and if you want, state that when you're finished, you expect to be done. Of course, you can politely add that if you aspire to go to the next level or tackle something else afterward, you'll certainly indicate that, and you'd be willing to discuss it. This way, you've established that your success does not imply that new demands can be automatically or inescapably imposed upon you.

○ **Consider the implications.** Think—what are the benefits and drawbacks of doing something well? Or not doing it at all? If you put your thoughts in writing, it might help you decide if you want to procrastinate or proceed.

○ **What's next?** If you're afraid that doing a task really well will inevitably lead to having to do more or harder tasks, why not find out exactly what these might be—ahead of time? That way, there won't be any surprises. Uncertainty can lead to procrastination. Knowing what's ahead can make getting there more motivating.

○ **Make it your choice!** Set the stage for the next set of demands by taking some control over what they might be. Co-create the expectations, or think through what you'd like them to be (assuming you complete the first ones successfully). Negotiate this so you can look forward to completing the first task *and* embarking on any subsequent ones.

○ **Share the vibe.** Be successful! And then, rather than dodging additional "work," share what you know by helping others or by taking a leadership role. It will make you feel good.

○ **"Dumbing-down" is not cool.** Sometimes, bright teens intentionally opt to take on less in order to indicate that they aren't as smart as people might think. Why? They may believe this will help them fit in better with others, or that they can evade excess work, or that their self-fulfillment does not depend on doing (or achieving) but on something else altogether. Whether you think this is sound reasoning or not, the reality is that deliberately opting out of opportunities to do, learn, participate, and share interferes with personal growth. It's like a form of self-sabotage. If you want to be the best version of yourself, don't try to be less, do less, or learn less. It will compromise your intelligence and hinder your ambition. Consider the consequences of that. It's far better to project that you're capable, and proud of it. Being smart is an advantage.[18] Don't flip off your personal light switch or undermine your smarts.

○ **Be gracious about excellence.** If you worry that others will be envious of your success, or think you're stuck up or showing off, make an effort to show some humility. Try not to be arrogant or boastful. You can achieve and enjoy success without being showy or conceited. Let others know that you admire what they're doing, too.

○ **You don't always have to achieve excellence.** Perhaps you're afraid that doing something really well will establish a very high standard that you'll have to meet for everything— and for always. This can lead to procrastination. Chat with the person setting the expectations, and talk about how you appreciate excellence but can't attain it all the time. Be truthful, and willing to try, and you will be respected for your honesty and effort.

· ·

In the whole scheme of things, success is something to cherish and strive toward. If you're fortunate enough to be successful in some areas of life, don't squander it. Aspire to be the best you can be—now. Why wait?

BUT…My feelings get in the way

Some feelings are just hard to manage. For example, anger, disappointment, fright, and guilt can make people so upset that they don't want to do anything. And, when people spend too much time trying to cope with these kinds of feelings, it leaves less time (and inclination and energy) to be able to devote to other activities. Strong feelings can frustrate, dampen spirits, lead to confusion, and derail initiative, all of which are likely to lead to procrastination and avoidance.

It's important to get your emotions under control so they don't interfere with your productivity. What happens to you, and what you achieve, has a lot to do with whether you can manage your emotions and get your stressors in check. You will accomplish more if you're able to think clearly and calmly.

Of course, you will have feelings about things, and it's actually good to have an emotional connection to whatever you have to do or learn. It makes it meaningful, and therefore easier to remember and to apply the information. Emotions and reason can work in harmony. Emotions can give you a boost, and excitement, happiness, empowerment, and other positive feelings provide a solid base for learning and action. Negative emotions (like sadness, fear, or embarrassment), however, can interfere with reasoning and the ability to focus on things such as new ideas or difficult tasks.

If you can keep your feelings in check, especially the negative ones, you'll be better able to concentrate on getting things done. So, think—what helps you feel calm?

There are many healthy ways to deal with emotions when they become pent up or start spiraling out of control. Perhaps you could make a list of different ways to release or to control emotions based on what's worked for you in the past. Then you can refer to this list whenever you need to. Ideas on such a list might include: punch a pillow, go for a walk, give or get a hug, swing, play with a pet, have a favorite snack, give yourself a compliment, jump on cushions, meditate, pray, exercise, blow bubbles, go swimming, or do something else you really like to do.

Here are some more tips to help you manage your emotions and become more productive.

. . . .

TIPS for when you procrastinate because your feelings interfere

○ **Acknowledge your feelings.** It's not good to ignore them. Talk about what you're feeling with someone you trust—maybe a family member, friend, or teacher. A big part of understanding your feelings has to do with becoming more aware of them.

○ **Express feelings through the arts.** If you don't feel like talking, consider other ways of expressing yourself. Drawing, journal writing, and playing music are all good emotional and communication outlets, and they can help you relax. They can also lead to meaningful discussions when you are ready to talk. Once you feel more at ease, you'll be better able to focus on whatever it is you have to do.

○ **Identify what you're feeling at different times.** Try to get a handle on what you feel right when you feel it, so you can pinpoint what's causing you to procrastinate. What do you feel at the outset of avoidance? (Possibly fear? Doubt? Self-reproach?) What do you feel when you are in the middle of procrastinating? (Possibly regret? Annoyance? Worry?) And, also, what do you feel when you *don't* procrastinate and accomplish things? (Possibly happiness? Satisfaction? Pride?) Being able to acknowledge and label feelings will help you to understand yourself better. It's a solid step toward managing your emotions.[19]

○ **Practice self-forgiveness.** Blaming yourself for procrastinating, or having negative thoughts about yourself, can further block your productivity. Say to yourself, "*I'm a capable person, and I can make good choices.*" And then make the choice not to feel ashamed or to scold yourself but instead to feel hopeful and take a step forward. Life is full of choices. How you value these, and what the outcomes will be, rests to a large extent upon your will and upon your attitude toward yourself.

○ **Deal with issues one by one.** Sometimes it feels like there's a lot of stuff to process, and so you get emotional. Maybe by yelling, or crying, or not being able to concentrate. Juggling too much is exhausting and difficult. When people get tired or upset, they often make poor decisions, or avoid doing things. Try to focus on just one specific situation or demand at a time. It's not necessary to start with a BIG step, take a little one.

○ **What's changeable?** If something in particular is causing you to have angry, sad, or other negative or uncomfortable feelings, pin down what it is. How can you change it or move it from your immediate environment so that you can get on with things? If a task or expectations are causing you to feel bad, think about whether it's the whole thing or just a portion of it. If you break it down, you might be able to get started on a part that you *can* manage comfortably.

○ **Calming influences.** Sometimes, toning down your surroundings can give you peace of mind. Too much stimulation is hard to handle when you're anxious or trying to deal with your feelings. Neutral colored rooms, uncluttered spaces, and fewer distractions can be soothing. Rubber squeeze balls or fidgety toys can help alleviate stress. Soft music and non-glare lighting are calming. You might relax by doodling, chewing gum, deep breathing, or walking (on a treadmill or elsewhere) for a few minutes. Coloring books have become very popular. Think about what calming influence might work for you.[20]

○ **How do others control their emotions?** Find out how other people (or maybe even characters you admire in books or movies) deal with emotions such as anger, or disappointment. What can you learn from them? Do they give up, or do they find some way to deal with their feelings so they can move on?

○ **Be happy.** Make time to play and have fun. Dance, sing, joke around with friends, and spend time doing the things you enjoy doing that make you happy. It will give you a sense of purpose, and strengthen not only your optimism but also your connections with the world around you. When you feel upbeat, you can turn that positivity into action. Comedian Amy Schumer has the right idea when she says, *"The moments that make life worth living are when things are at their worst and you find a way to laugh."*

○ **Venting can be beneficial.** It's okay to take time to cry, laugh, or stomp. Try breathing exercises, or physical exertion (squeeze a pillow, rip paper, hit a punching bag, or scrunch empty pop cans if you feel like you want to clobber someone or something)—and unwind. These actions are a way to let the stress out, like when steam escapes through the spout or escape valve of the kettle when the water starts to boil. It's a natural response, and venting will help you settle down and compose yourself, and then you can refocus afterward.

• •

There are plenty of websites and books that deal with emotional intelligence—sometimes called EI or EQ (emotional quotient). Have a look at the readily available information for some useful tips.[21] Many of these resources are targeted for kids of specific ages or academic levels (elementary, middle school, high school, or college). A school guidance counselor may also be able to recommend some useful books or other materials.

BUT...What if it's not perfect?

Let's begin this section with the premise that nobody and nothing is really perfect, and then move on from there.

People and things have flaws. They may be in different areas, in different proportions, and at different times. Some may be more visible than others, and some may be concealed. Perfection is elusive; imperfection is inevitable. Life is like that. Yet, it can be difficult to allow yourself to accept "good enough" rather than perfection. (This is a major theme of Lisa Van Gemert's book, *Perfectionism: A Practical Guide to Managing "Never Good Enough."*[22])

I've worked with thousands of capable, intelligent, and creative children and adults, and I've heard comments like these:

○ *"If I can't do it perfectly, then it's not worth doing at all."*

○ *"They expect me to do things perfectly. I can't. So, I'm not even going to try."*

○ *"If it's not perfect, then people will laugh at me."*

○ *"I did it perfectly last time, but it's harder now. I'd rather quit while I'm ahead."*

Each of these four comments about perfectionism has a different underlying rationale. Let's consider the examples briefly, one at time, looking at the messages, and posing a few quick questions (or buts…) as we think about each of them.

The first comment is: *"If I can't do it perfectly, then it's not worth doing at all."* This view of perfectionism has to do with extremely high and unrealistic personal standards or *self-imposed expectations.* This perfectionist thinks that accomplishments have to be 100 percent correct, and if that's not likely to happen, then why bother? But…Why does the particular task have to be done perfectly? What will happen if the end result is not perfect? Why not focus instead on the value of what can be learned?

The second comment is: *"They expect me to do things perfectly. I can't. So, I'm not even going to try."* These words relate to *other-oriented expectations*—perhaps set by parents, teachers, or friends. This kind of perfectionist thinks that it's impossible to do the task the way people think it should be done (that is, perfectly). Rather than appearing to be incapable, the person gives up, by procrastinating or by avoiding the task altogether. But…Why not discuss the expectations and determine if they're really rigid or if there's some flexibility? How can the task and the expectations be subdivided into stages or manageable segments? What kind of help is available when or if the demands become too challenging?

The third comment is: *"If it's not perfect, then people will laugh at me."* This procrastinator has *fears about social implications* such as embarrassment, teasing, or rejection. Nobody wants to feel that others might think less of him for trying something and then not being able to excel at it. But… Why do the opinions of other people matter so much? Why is self-worth dependent upon this particular task being completed perfectly? What behaviors and responses work most effectively in circumstances when people criticize, bully, or tease others? (Look for resources and tips in the endnotes.[23])

The fourth comment is: *"I did it perfectly last time, but it's harder now. I'd rather quit while I'm ahead."* This is a *surrender* of sorts. This perfectionist is bowing out, unwilling to take a chance, lose control, or trust that success is reachable yet again, and is thereby relinquishing the opportunity to progress further. But… Why? What's the worst that could happen? What will be gained by giving up? Why not start the task slowly, and think positively?

If you want to create new ideas, or extend your ability, begin with what you know and can already do, and move on from there. Taking a few small steps using the knowledge and skills that are familiar to you is like building a bridge—you need firm footings and a solid foundation for it to be strong enough. Whether it's math, volleyball, designing a lab experiment, chess, or something else, ascertain what you already understand and ask yourself, *"What else do I need to know in order to progress further?"* Then stick with it as long as you can. (Take a break when you need to.)

What's perfect anyhow? Is it a gold-medal error-free perfor-mance? Do you procrastinate because you're not sure you can attain that? Frankly, there are few gold medals, and life is full of stumbling blocks. Simone Biles, a gymnast who *has* won gold—in fact, she won a combined total of 19 Olympic and World Championship medals, all before the age of 20—says quite simply, *"I take things one step at a time."* She advises, *"Always work hard, and have fun in what you do."*

There's a lot to be said for enjoyment and involvement. You can still consider yourself very successful at math, volleyball, an experiment, chess, playing the violin, baking, or..., even if you don't get a trophy or you make mistakes. You can pat yourself on the back and be proud!

Perfectionists are often so focused on avoiding mistakes and on final outcomes that they miss thinking about the pleasure, pride, and personal growth that can be attained along the way. After all, *"If you only do what you can do, you will never be more than you are now."*[24] Here are some suggestions for perfectionists.

• •

TIPS for when you procrastinate because of perfectionism

○ **Re-evaluate expectations.** Regardless of who is setting the expectations (you or someone else), make sure they're not outrageously high. Strive toward realistic standards. They should be fair and manageable. If expectations are too lofty, revisit them with the idea of bringing them within reach.

○ **Differentiate between success and perfectionism.** Success is achievable, whereas perfection is not likely to be a sensible end-goal. What is "good enough" for you? Give yourself room to grow.[25] Thoughtful and creative work can still elicit feelings of pride and satisfaction, even when not perfect. Psychologist Thomas Greenspon, who writes extensively about perfectionism, reminds us how the inventor of the light bulb engaged in guesswork, and surmounted failures and difficulties. *"If Edison had been paralyzed by perfectionism—by the fear of making a mistake—we might all still be living in the dark."* [26]

○ Make a mistake on porpoise. Just to see what happens. It's okay. Take a deep breath. Don't be hard on yourself just because something you've done is not error free. Some people intentionally try to make mistakes just to help themselves overcome their perfectionism.

○ **Become more aware of others.** Who do you admire? Think of family members, friends, or even celebrities. Can you think of any flaws they have? Yet, you admire them anyway! If you accept their imperfections, consider how you might be more accepting of your own flaws, or any mistakes you might make.

○ **Commit—then relax.** Albert Einstein said, *"It's not that I'm so smart, it's just that I stay with problems longer."* It's great to dig in and persist until you've completed a task. However, there's no shame in starting it, doing it to the best of your ability, and then setting it aside. Perhaps you'll come back to it. Perhaps you won't. But maybe in a while you'll see it in a new light, or come up with a more creative approach. Einstein didn't solve his "problems" in one sitting. Nor did he actually resolve all the many challenges he tackled. (In fact, physicists today are still working to find out whether or not some of his theories can be proved.) Cut yourself some slack and don't expect flawless outcomes. Think, *"I'll do it now, and maybe improve upon it or make it more exact later."*

○ **How is perfectionism affecting you?** What toll is perfectionism taking on your body and on your mind? Do you feel stressed? Depressed? Worn out from taking on too much? Unable to enjoy time with your friends and family because you're too focused on getting everything perfect? Do you ever burst into tears that just keep on coming, or have difficulty sleeping because you're too worked up about things having to be exactly right? You may need professional help if perfectionism is interfering with your health or your daily life. Speak to a trusted adult or call a crisis hotline in your community.

○ **Is your goal reachable?** If a goal isn't attainable, then there's little incentive to strive for it. So, find a way to make it reachable. For example, let's say you have to take a series of selfies for the school yearbook but you want them to be "perfect." Otherwise you choose not to submit any at all. Think about who can help you get things like lighting, angles, and composition exactly the way you'd like them to be. Or check out possible resources, such as going online and learning how artistic photographers get pictures to look "just so." Set aside a small amount of time to practice the techniques so it will be easier from then on. Remember, in instances like this you're not trying to solve a world crisis or walk on Mars. You're simply trying to find a way to do something that's quite doable once you acquire the skills—so you won't be unnecessarily frustrated by it, and you can get on with your day.

○ **A hole-in-one?** Seriously? People play golf for years and years and years, and never get a "perfect" shot. If they do get a hole-in-one, it's a bonus. The real pleasure is in playing the game.

○ **Don't compare yourself to others who seem to be perfect.** Other people's so-called perfection may not be real. For example, the images and various achievements you see posted on social media might look great but they don't necessarily reveal the whole truth. People who are interested in promoting themselves seldom expose issues or flaws. Instead of comparing yourself to others (looks, accomplishments, or other aspects of their lives), whether online or in person, channel your energy in positive ways and go about living your own life. You are uniquely you! Singer Ariana Grande says, *"Be happy with being you. Love your flaws. Own your quirks. And know that you are just as perfect as anyone else, exactly as you are."*

○ **What else matters?** Perfectionism isn't the most important thing to strive for. Think about what else you could focus on, that you can attain and that will help you to feel positive about yourself. For example, being a trusted friend, showing compassion, and helping others. Appreciate yourself for who you are and what you can do, even if it's not done to perfection. You don't have to be a whiz or get straight As to be a good person.

○ **First place is not always the best place.** There's one place in front, or at the top of the heap; it reflects perfection and all the rest trail behind. Or, so you may think. However, the middle range is not inferior or second-rate. That's where you'll find opportunity to grow, practice, experiment, and learn—all of which will enable you to strive with renewed vigor and know-how next time. So, if you procrastinate because you don't think you can lead the pack, you will miss out on those opportunities.

○ **Imperfection as a threat?** If you don't do things perfectly, and it's not a direct threat to your health or safety, then what's the big deal? Yes, you have to use a car seat belt properly; and yes, you have to take medicine exactly as the doctor says; and yes, there's a smart way to navigate the shore if stinging jellyfish are washing up on the beach. But, when it comes to doing homework, practicing guitar, making the bed, folding laundry, or other daily responsibilities, there's likely only very minimal danger if the task is not competed perfectly. So, get comfortable, and get started!

. . . .

If perfectionism is a problem for you, then try to face potential defects or imperfections slowly, one incident or concern at a time. For example, if someone gives you a birthday cake, and the writing on top is not precise—there's a smudge, or a glob of icing, or the letters in the message are poorly formed—think past that. Focus instead on the kindness of the person who gave you the cake, the effort put forth by the baker, the deliciousness of the cake, and the joy of celebrating with others. Why let imperfect icing deter you from the pleasures you can experience? And, similarly, why let real or possible flaws impede your progress in life? Be a *doer,* even though the process and the results are not apt to be perfect. Concentrate on the positive and on what you can achieve.

BUT...I don't feel well

Sometimes we're low on sleep, energy, nutrition, or exercise, and as a result we might not want to do anything. We don't feel up to it. We may procrastinate. That's understandable.

Bodies are like transmitters, sending messages that can influence decision-making, energy levels, emotions, and more. For example, when the body receives proper nutrition, it's energized, and ready for action; whereas hunger, thirst, or eating or drinking the wrong foods (such as too much "fast sugar") make it hard to concentrate. And, when people feel tired or unhealthy, they tend to tune out and become less responsive to what's around them.

If you find you're procrastinating because of sickness, poor dietary choices, insufficient sleep, or lack of physical activity, there are steps you can take to help yourself.

• •

TIPS for when you procrastinate because you aren't feeling well

○ **Pay attention to your body.** Body self-awareness means being alert to signs such as fatigue, lack of energy, stress, and other indicators that you're not feeling well. If you're having trouble meeting challenges because of reasons relating to these health indicators, it's important to acknowledge and then address them—with sleep, medicine, relaxation, or whatever else you require, depending on the circumstances.

○ **Eat well.** Have a good breakfast. If you start the day off with a sensible meal, you'll be better prepared to handle the morning's activities than if you skip breakfast, or have sugary food or sodas. Consider eating protein-rich foods like eggs, cheese, nuts, and yogurt. These will prevent you from feeling hungry as quickly. Wholesome meals will help you maintain strong energy levels so you can function effectively throughout the day. Think about your food choices, and develop healthy eating habits.

○ **Track your energy levels.** Keep track of how you feel at different times of the day and night. When do you tend to be energized? When are you in a slump? If you can verify when you are most efficient, you can use this information to help you to determine your "prime times," develop a productive routine, and stop procrastinating.

○ **Do you need to see a doctor?** If your health is endangered, then it's smart to seek the advice of a doctor or a trained health professional so you can feel better and get back on track.

○ **Use your brain to know yourself.** The executive function part of your brain is like its control center. It looks after "processing" jobs, such as planning, initiating, responding, and focusing on tasks. If you pay attention to your own functioning, you can learn from that. For example, what happens when something is overwhelming and you procrastinate? Do you tune out? Do you yell? Do you cry? Bodily awareness can help you become more attuned to how you react to challenge, as well as the kinds of strategies that seem to calm you down. Your brain is constantly undergoing changes, so you can break old patterns and develop new ways of functioning—and this includes the possibility of developing more efficient approaches and changing patterns of delay.

○ **Sleep is important.** There is no doubt that people work best when they've had adequate sleep. The brain needs time to rest, to consolidate ideas, and to process information. Being tired can affect your mood, behavior, appetite, energy, and focus. Productivity declines when you're deprived of sleep, so make sure you get enough rest, and on a regular basis.

○ **Pause to consider HALT.** These four letters stand for hunger, anger, loneliness, and tiredness. These are called primary concerns, and if they're not managed, it can lead to stress. Many counselors and treatment centers offer programs that suggest ways of tending to these needs. Be sure to speak to a trusted adult to get help if you feel that your primary needs are not being met.

○ **Everybody experiences ups and downs.** Everyone has good days and bad days, times when they feel great, and times when they feel low—and unproductive. By recognizing and balancing out these times, then if you're not at your best one day you can compensate for it the next.[27] Find your own bio-rhythm, like the ebb and flow of the tides, and resolve to work with it. You can note your moods, and when you're feeling less healthy—and make an effort to discern "why." Take advantage of intervals when you're energetic, but also look for ways to boost your well-being and increase your energy levels when you're below par (and catch yourself procrastinating). Thoughtful consideration of your ups and downs, perhaps by writing them in a daily journal, can help you learn to level them off over time.

• •

A framework for action is little more than an empty plan if your ability to function breaks down. The power to go beyond intentions and to get things done (as opposed to procrastinating) can depend on your wellness. Your physical and emotional well-being really do matter, so try to pay attention to them.

BUT...I'm confused

Everyone has experienced confusion at some point. Toddlers learning to walk have no idea where to head first. Children in the playground want to run every which way. As people get older, they have more and more places they *have* to go, and more and more things they *have* to do, and life is one big whirl of activity. Things do get confusing.

I understand confusion. I have an extremely poor sense of direction and get mixed up when people tell me to head east or west. I even have to think carefully about left and right. However, I've learned to compensate by using coping skills. I get specific directions and write them down. I use technology, like GPS. I reflect upon my past experiences and what I already know, and think about familiar visual markers that will help me position my whereabouts for the future. I plan where I'm going ahead of time so I won't be muddled or flustered. I ask for additional directions if I do get lost. And, I encourage people to please have patience with me as I experiment with additional strategies to try and sharpen my directional sense. (Some work, some don't.)

What I *don't* do is stay in one place. That would be a simple, but not particularly helpful, response to my state of confusion. If I were to avoid going places, or if I were to procrastinate in getting started, I would end up going pretty much nowhere. And what good is that? Sometimes I take a wrong step (or road, or turn) and I wind up in the wrong place. I learn from that. And, sometimes my missteps take me in new directions or, in the long run, I ultimately end up at the right destination. I learn from that, too. The point is, I keep trying, and keep moving. I may be uncomfortable about my confusion, but I don't let it hinder or stop me.

Despite this example, you might think that confusion seems like a legitimate reason for putting things off. Let's say you have difficulty with instructions, or finding and sifting through a load of resource materials, or you're being slammed with too many things at once. Any or all of these examples can generate confusion, and then procrastination. Whatever the source of your confusion, there are strategies that will help smooth the way, making the task that you confront less complicated and more manageable.

U.S. President John F. Kennedy said, *"Efforts and courage are not enough without purpose and direction,"* and you can get past confusion by harnessing purpose and acquiring direction. In doing so, you will gain forward momentum. Here are some tips to help you do that.

· ·

TIPS for when you procrastinate because you're confused

○ **Get exact instructions.** If you record the instructions, and therefore have a log of the expectations, it will be easier to refer back to them. Number the steps. Be precise. Keep the information where you can see it.

○ **Do you rush?** Try to be patient with yourself. Take a few moments to cool off. If you're feeling confused, rushing may make things worse because you can accidentally jumble things and become even more confused.

○ **Take two steps forward—and sometimes one step back or sideways.** Be prepared to pause or possibly readjust as you move forward with whatever it is you're doing or working on. Success doesn't generally happen by way of a straight line from start to finish. There are often twists, turns, and occurrences that will make you stop and think. That's not necessarily a bad thing. You may make some surprising or exciting discoveries as you advance.

○ **Accept your confusion!** You can even try to enjoy confusion to some extent because it can push you to strive harder and give you opportunities to learn to problem-solve.

○ **There's more than one way to get somewhere.** Find *your* way. It may take longer, or be more or less interesting, or be laden with challenges, but the important thing is to take that first step. Your way may not be the same as someone else's, but who's to say which route is the best?

○ **Confusion is like a puzzle waiting to be solved.** Puzzle pieces laid out in a jumble look daunting. Sorting them out requires time and patience, and trial and error, and a willingness to confront the challenge. Once you start, and things begin to take shape, there's satisfaction in the process. Procrastination does not yield satisfaction. Why not find a few bits that fit together, and use that as a starting point for success?

○ **Confusion is part of the real world.** The best chefs work in kitchens that often appear to be bustling, hectic, and confusing places. Writers often have desks covered haphazardly with notes and drafts. Florists create beautiful bouquets and arrangements amidst workbenches piled with leaves, twigs, ribbons, and discarded blooms. None of these doers avoids the confusion, nor do they let it get them down. They recognize that it's an inevitable aspect of their creative environment, and they go about their business—productively. As artist Paul Cezanne said, *"We live in a rainbow of chaos."* If you embrace confusion, you may even find that it becomes a trigger for creative expression!

○ **Simplify.** If something seems too complicated, break it down into words or actions that make sense to you. You can also ask a few intelligent questions to get information you need. For example, if someone told you they were studying xixianykus zhangi you'd probably be confused. You might even tune out and avoid chatting with them because xixianykus zhangi doesn't register as something you recognize or understand. Is it a foreign language? An athletic pursuit? A math concept? (Actually, it's a kind of dinosaur. Quite small, and probably covered with feathers!) Once you get past the initial confusion, you're set to become interested in finding out more.

• •

We all handle confusion differently. That's because we experience different types of confusion, we have different tolerance levels, and we have different dispositions—that is, states of mind or ways of thinking that cause us to think or act in certain ways. You might procrastinate, or avoid something confusing. Or you might use the strategies listed above to help you get past mystified muddling, and move into constructive action mode. It's up to you.

BUT...I'm lazy

We all have times when we feel like doing nothing. It may be a sun-drenched morning, a cloud-filled afternoon, or a rain-driven evening. Any time, any month, any season. Laziness is defined as sluggishness, or not wanting to work. It's more than just a feeling though; it's an absence of action. It's a choice. While the rest of the world hums with activity, there are times when you would rather take a pass. Like a heavy-eyed dog, not quite ready to chase that squirrel. Or a car with the motor running but going nowhere. For now...

"Zoning out" can take various forms. Gazing, wandering, daydreaming—these are seemingly indicators of laziness. And yet, the mind is always active; the brain is whirring. Being lazy provides opportunities to have those "aha! moments" that might not come when you're too busy paying attention to details or doing chores. When we laze about, we rest, conserve energy, and reserve the right to do things later, often by procrastinating.

Laziness is commonly thought to be a negative response to responsibility, a cop out. However, laziness can give the body a chance to re-energize so there will be stored up reserves of enthusiasm and vigor to call upon when needed. Remember, a lull often precedes a storm. And, a hectic lifestyle that's filled to the max with multi-tasking and pressures is not necessarily the most efficient. A bit of laziness can sometimes be a welcome relief.

There is also some basis to the argument that lazy people often contribute a lot to the world—in their own way, and in their own good time. Scientists, artists, authors, and others may appear lazy to people in their fields when they're not "working." But... They may be mentally generating solutions, designs, or story lines! What constitutes good work habits will differ from one person to another. For example, a person who *seems* productively occupied may actually be busy with unimportant or shallow tasks, whereas someone who *seems* sluggish may be engaged in deep thinking.

So, what if you're actively answering a long stream of mindless e-mails? It may not look like laziness, but you may actually be procrastinating from doing something more meaningful. And, what if you're just sitting quietly while thinking about creative ideas for a writing assignment? That may not be laziness at all. I sat outside today and watched the birds in my backyard, while mulling over what I was going to include in my next workshop talk. Anyone looking over the fence would have thought, *"She's being lazy!"*

The truth lies in whether a person is spending time doing something that matters. If you're acting purposefully and you're engaged in a worthwhile task or activity, then chances are you aren't really being lazy. However, if you procrastinate because you *are* lazy (from time to time, or more frequently), and you want to deal with your laziness, then the following tips might be helpful for you.

TIPS for when you procrastinate because you're lazy

○ **Feeble excuses are…well…feeble.** Laziness is not sinful. But nobody likes to hear pitiful explanations. Take ownership of your laziness. If you choose to press the snooze button over and over, or lie in a hammock and swing gently in the breeze for a long while, that's your call. But, lame excuses can be annoying to other people. Just take the time you need to build up the energy and the desire that you require in order to do what you have to do. Then do it.

○ **Think of ambition as an outgrowth of laziness.** Try to keep lazy times short, and if possible offset them by using some of those relaxing moments to focus on what you can accomplish once you actually get started. The most skilled athletes think about their responsibilities and live up to them, but they don't think about their sports or practice 24/7. They enjoy leisure time and occasional lazy days, too. Then, they flip the "action switch."

○ **Reading is not laziness.** Quiet times spent reading, reflecting, or thinking about how you might proceed are productive. What might look like laziness on the outside may in fact be busyness or measured pre-productivity and planning on the inside.

○ **Be aware of your state of mind.** Is laziness your way of coping with unhappiness, anger, fear, disappointment, or some other feeling that's hard to handle? Can you acknowledge and calm that feeling? If your "laziness" takes the form of curling up in a ball, not talking to anyone, staying in bed for days on end, or not looking after yourself properly, then you may need some professional help. A caring adult can direct you to someone who can determine if you're confusing laziness with depression or other issues that might require counseling or medical attention.[28]

○ **Higher purpose.** People can be motivated by a sense of purpose, whether it applies to themselves, or whether they see something as possibly extending further and somehow affecting the greater good. For example, thinking that your actions might help shape the future, have a positive impact on others, or make a difference, can be inspiring and propel you to act. Laziness, by definition, is idleness, or inaction. Ask yourself, "*What's the* purpose *of my procrastinating or just lazing about?*" If you can't come up with a good (productive) answer, then think about being more purposeful—and choose to act upon it. Purposefulness is like a virtual vitamin that will strengthen your intent and productivity, and it will help keep procrastination at bay.

○ **Napping is not laziness.** Studies show that a nap is a good way to revitalize the body and mind. Naps can help lower blood pressure, improve moods, and make people more tolerant of frustration. After a nap, people tend to be more alert and responsive, not to mention rested.

○ **Flexible hours have pluses.** When are you at your best? Maybe it's during the evening—whereas after school or early morning hours are not peak times for you to get things done, and you prefer to be lazy. There are many reasons why you may feel tired or, conversely, alert at different times of the day or night. Your circadian rhythm is a key factor. It's the 24-hour clock operating within your brain, and it affects your sleep and wake cycles, including when you experience swings in tiredness and alertness.[29] Find your optimal, most energy-filled time of day (or night), and then try to use it wisely. The "work rhythm" most suited to your productivity may not be the same as your friends', and it may not align with the preferences of your family, school, coach or workplace. So, try to be considerate of others. Remember that when you choose to stay up till 2:00am working on a paper (because you were lazy, or procrastinated, or for some other reason), you still need to be up for school or work in the morning. As long as you deliver results, then perhaps you can consider lazy or idle intervals as earned breaks.

○ **How lazy are you?** Keep track of how much time you laze about per day, or maybe per week. If you discover that you're wasting a great deal of time on a regular basis, consider the implications. It may motivate you to be more proactive.

○ **A lazy approach may be the smartest one.** Lazy people sometimes find the simplest or most straightforward method of tackling problems. They laze about, and then wham! They get going. All things considered, a work-laden or complicated way of doing something is not necessarily the most efficient. Taking a shortcut, or saving yourself the trouble of doing something the hard way may appear to be laziness, when it may, in fact, be strategic, productive, and resourceful.

○ **Transition times may promote laziness.** Like the water that splashes in and out of a harbor, our days have different shifts and patterns. For example, you may have to switch from home to school to extra-curricular programs to home again, and all of this involves juggling responsibilities, and several changes of place and pace. You may find it helpful to pop a bit of good old-fashioned laziness into your day as you move from one activity to another. It's fine to have a couple of lazy recesses or intermission times. (However, can you then balance these with more productive or accelerated times?)

○ **What's lazy anyhow?** Watching television? Playing video games? Doing a puzzle? Checking the Internet? Listening to music? Waiting for the spark of a creative idea? Each of these may be presumed by some to be "a waste of time," yet they might also be opportunities for renewing energy, or for learning. Everyone has a different sense of what laziness is, and isn't. Labels can be misleading, and finger pointing can be hurtful, so be careful before calling anyone lazy. Their behavior may be something else altogether, including a way of coping with being maxed out, or a sensible prelude to productivity.

• •

People who procrastinate may appear to be slow to start or act, or they may be readying themselves to tackle what lies ahead. Taking an independent, relaxed, or unusual approach can also work out for the best, even if others misinterpret this as laziness. It's good for you to function in a way that's comfortable, but at the same time, you can resolve to be successful, too. Think about the story of the tortoise and the hare. The tortoise not only reached the finish line, he got there first. He was slow, perhaps to the point of being *perceived* as lazy, but he was actually steady and focused. The hare, on the other hand, was fast, but he really *was* lazy, as well as overconfident. He lost the race.

BUT...I have to look at the BIG picture first

You might be the kind of person who doesn't like to begin a task unless you're able to envision the whole thing from beginning to end, so you'll know if you can comfortably achieve it. You might be afraid of challenges that would occur part way through. Or, something surprising might come up. Or, there may be things you need in order to get the job done, and you want to be properly prepared. Perhaps the task is large, and you find it's easier to pre-pare a timeline so you can view the expectations in full. Or there may be other reasons why you want to see "the whole staircase," not just the first step.[30] And so you may choose to procrastinate, for logical reasons.

For example, you have to review a lengthy instruction hand-book before you can take your driver's test. There's also a prelimi-nary online quiz on road signs, rules, speed limits, fines, and more. Plus, in addition to taking the written exam, you have to practice driving on streets and on the highway, and spend time going over tricky maneuvers like parallel parking and three-point turns. Then, you have to take an on-road exam. It all seems very daunting—and anyway, you may be saying to yourself, "*Why should I do all that? There are cars that drive themselves so I don't have to!*"

True. However, by discounting the need to learn to drive, and by procrastinating, you are sidestepping a skill. Although self-driv-ing cars are a reality, they are pretty rare and the technology is still evolving. It probably makes more sense to start reading that driving manual (taking the first step, and setting aside the full magnitude of the many driver's test prerequisites) because the likelihood of your having a driverless car in the near future is wishful thinking.

Procrastination can become problematic if you allow the BIG picture to distort your perspective. You may end up deceiving your-self, fail to take an important action, miss out on valuable learning experiences, and perhaps also inconvenience others. You may not be able to get started in a timely enough manner to get to everything that needs to get done. You may discover that the BIG picture ends up getting bigger the longer you put it off. Then, as you become increasingly discouraged by the largeness of what lies ahead, you avoid it altogether. As time goes by, you may get more and more upset so that the BIG picture results in BIG feelings such as dismay, shame, embarrassment, or guilt—and these feelings can be stressful.

Putting things off so you can see the entire scope of a task may seem strategic, but when you stop to think about it, a BIG task is really just a bunch of smaller ones. If you view them as bite-sized pieces, instead of a huge plate full of stuff, it will be easier to digest.

No one can eat an entire pizza in one swallow. You might want to *see* the whole thing, but regardless of what it looks like in its entirety, it will taste the same whether you see it or not, and the truth is that you still have to tackle it one piece at a time. And, as you do, the BIGness becomes less big…

If you have difficulty getting past the BIG picture approach, and you procrastinate, you could consider the suggestions below.

• •

TIPS for when you procrastinate because you want the BIG picture

○ **Block your time well.** Use an agenda or calendar, or create an itinerary. Give yourself time to do the initial overview of everything that you want to do, and then be sure to block off enough time to do the task itself. You don't want to run out of time before you're able to complete it.

○ **Who else should you consider?** If a slow start is going to affect other people in some way (for example, if they're counting on you), be sure to connect with them so they're aware that you're looking at the BIG picture, and know what you have planned.

○ **What if the picture looks way too BIG?** Ask for help. Break it down. See if you can get a longer time period for completion. You can insert a "catch up" day or a "time out" segment into your plan as a safeguard, just in case you need it.

○ **Ask smart questions.** If you intend to get a realistic and thorough overview of the situation, think about what information you may need, and how you might be able to get it as quickly as possible so you can proceed.

○ **Join up with others.** Can you share the BIG task? Maybe you can join a study group, or hook up with friends. If three or four people design a historical timeline, review a play, or weed a lawn, the job gets divided up and becomes more manageable. You can share responsibilities, and encourage and support one another.

○ **Slot in the R's—re-envision, repair, revise, or redo.** Any plans that take into account the BIG picture should also leave time to remedy the results. The final product or end goal won't seem as tough, and you'll feel more confident if you know you've set aside the opportunity to fix, edit, and fine-tune results.

○ **Have faith in your ability to overcome a high hurdle.** Give yourself a pep talk, going over what you have to do. Think positively about the path you'll have to take to get there. Then, take it. The phrase "self-talk" refers to the words people use to convince or coach themselves into action, by reviewing what they have to focus on, and how they intend to proceed, one step at a time. Self-talk can be a useful way to give yourself a boost.[31]

○ **Use mental imagery.** Close your eyes and picture yourself doing just the first one or two things that need to get done on the way to completing the BIG task. In the same way that you're reading a single page of this book at a time (and may not even need to go through the entire book), imagine tackling just one aspect of the task you have to confront— and then taking a breather before making a fresh start and tackling another, and another, as you "see" fit.

○ **The BIG picture is important.** You shouldn't have to make excuses for wanting to appreciate and become knowledge-able about the "whole package." Instead, arrange it so that you have an opportunity to do so, and also opportunities to do the different bits and pieces of the task, and meet the necessary expectations. If you're going to procrastinate in order to get a better feel for what lies ahead, then think about that as being a strategic part of your action plan—not as a way to avoid it. Slot the necessary reflection time (or time to picture all the steps) into your agenda, and then move on with determination to reach your goal.

• •

The BIG picture might involve you thinking about some of the many personal considerations I've presented in this past chapter. However, there are also various skill-related reasons why people procrastinate. Some of these may apply to you, and they could hinder your productivity and success. In the next chapter, I discuss several of these skill-related reasons, and suggest strategies, too. They can help you to stop procrastinating and gain forward momentum.

CHAPTER 3

Skill-Related Reasons for Procrastination: What Are Your BUTS?

"Fortune favors the prepared mind."
~ Louis Pasteur (scientist)

BUT...I'm disorganized

Concentration. Rock climbing. Public speaking. Cooking. Organization. Self-discipline. Tap dancing. Whistling. Each of these is an acquired skill. Different skills are important to different people, and there are countless skills that people can learn—and then learn to strengthen.

If you procrastinate because you have a hard time with a particular skill, it would be a good idea to think about how you might develop that skill with training and practice. (Or if you'd prefer to embark on another skill, how you might make that happen.)

Organization is listed above because it is a skill. Many people believe that lack of organization leads to chaos and reduced productivity. Certainly, disorganization can result in wasted time (where are my things?), frustration (seriously, where are my things??) and self-reproach (I'm so bad at this; what's wrong with me that I can't find my things???). However, there is a hidden silver lining. According to author A. A. Milne, *"One of the advantages of being disorderly is that one is constantly making exciting discoveries."* Of course, you have to be willing to poke through the muddle and remain optimistic. Organization does not simply happen in a whoosh, or by accident. It takes practice, and it involves various and specific tasks such as straightening, discarding, filing, folding, replacing, and combining stuff. It requires time. And procrastinators may not want to invest the necessary effort that's required in order to get organized.

If organization is a problem for you, then you may believe that you are not ready to do something, or that you don't have enough control of how to go about accomplishing it. Perhaps you have certain habits or methods of doing things that leave you feeling poorly equipped or unprepared. Information, paper, messages, or commitments can pile up. You may want more time to deal with everything—or one specific thing—and so you procrastinate.

Disorganization is likely to interfere with many aspects of your life, including causing you to dither or delay, but you can get past it with some strategic planning.

• •
TIPS for when you procrastinate because you are disorganized

○ **Gather stuff together.** If you're about to tackle a task, first make sure you have the materials, space, and resources you need. A computer, a quiet corner, paper, duct tape, a bottle of water—whatever it might be. You don't want to be scrambling around unnecessarily part way through whatever it is that you're expected to do.

○ **What's missing?** Make a checklist, or review what you've gathered together. Then go over it to see if anything is missing.

○ **Declutter.** Set aside time to get rid of unnecessary stuff. It just gets in the way and makes it more challenging for you to get your hands on what you need, when you need it. As you proceed, think carefully about what you don't use. Streamline, pitch, recycle, have a garage sale, or give away items that might be of use to others. You never know, you might even find something vintage, unexpected, or valuable within the clutter.

○ **Mental clutter?** While we're on the subject of clutter, there's such a thing as mental clutter. It's the jumble of stuff like hopes, embarrassment, grudges, anger, regrets, and mismatched beliefs you have about yourself, others, and life that are whirling around in your head. These thoughts and feelings may no longer apply or fit with the way you think, and if you hold on to them, they can sap your energy and interfere with your ability to focus. Clear your mind by getting rid of mental clutter so you can concentrate on what matters now.

○ **Neatness is not overrated.** When things are scattered about, like heaped on an untidy desk, or strewn in a messy room, it's difficult to feel organized. Try bringing order to the disorder, even if it's only on the surface or by straightening a few things at a time. Go through one drawer. One shelf. One corner. It will add up. And, as a bonus, it will bring you a sense of satisfaction. (See the goal-setting information in the next section of this book for more ideas about this.)

○ **There are many useful products.** Agendas, planners, and calendars are pretty basic. Many are in the form of apps that you can download on your tablets or cell phones. Here are some other everyday items that can help you get organized: paper clips, markers, shelving units, binders, boxes, baskets, bags, file folders, post-it notes, alligator clips, fabric cubbies, hanging racks, and under the bed storage containers. What else might work for you? What other storage spots can you find for putting things away?

○ **Develop a routine.** Place things like keys, phones, gloves, sunglasses, or backpacks in the same location so you'll know where to find them and won't have to go searching. Keep instructions or subject-specific notes in convenient spots so you'll remember where they are. Consider creative color-coding or labeling options. Have a set time of day to do routine tasks like getting your backpack in order, or checking out snack options.

○ **Keep things you need most close by.** There are some things you always tend to use, like keys or glasses or a favorite hat. Put them where you can get at them easily. Be consistent.

○ **Welcome ideas.** Ask people you know what strategies they use to get organized. What advice can they share? For example, how do they prepare for complicated tasks? How do they maximize use of nooks and crannies? Where do they stash the things they need or value? How do they deal with eliminating unnecessary items?

○ **Prioritize**. When ideas, things, or commitments accumulate, pay attention to what's most important, and focus on that. Don't neglect other demands that are piling up, but plan how and when you can get to them. Use your agenda.

○ **Itineraries are useful**. An itinerary is like a time map, and it can help you get where you have to be when you have to be there, so that you can do what you have to do once you arrive. It may be meeting someone, or getting ready for team practice, or being on time for dinner. If you don't work out your timelines strategically, you can end up losing time before you realize it. And, it becomes hard to get back on schedule. An itinerary will help you track time, so you can use it wisely, and avoid delay. However, be realistic when you estimate the amount of time you will need to do things. And, include intervals for gathering your belongings, traveling from place to place, and other typical in-between activities. An itinerary works if you're willing to stick to it, and if you don't allow yourself to be distracted. Remember, the better you become at adhering to schedules and appreciating time, the less you'll be inclined to procrastinate because you'll know that time is valuable and shouldn't be wasted.

○ **Sloppiness is unsettling.** If you rush and do things half-heartedly now, you may be sorry later. If you find yourself rushing toward a deadline, see if there's some flexibility. Take pride in a job well done.

○ **Block off time regularly for the purpose of keeping yourself organized.** Devote a few minutes—say ten or fifteen—daily; or maybe a half hour weekly. Set it aside as organization time. Stay with it. Make it matter by making a conscious effort to avoid distractions and interruptions.

• •

Nobody is born knowing how to be organized. It's a skill that people choose to develop (like rock climbing or tap dancing). Some skills are going to be more useful to you, so there is decision-making involved. Do you want to be organized, or disorganized? If disorganization is a factor in your procrastination, and you tend to put things off (or even forget to do them) because of it, then organization is probably a skill worth acquiring. Developing this skill can be a reasonable goal. To learn more about setting goals, read on.

BUT...I have trouble setting goals

Author C. S. Lewis wrote, *"You are never too old to set another goal or to dream a new dream."*[32] By the way, you're never too young, either. However, setting good goals can be tricky. And, goals are created in different ways, at different times, and for different reasons.

The best goals are specific and reachable. For example, getting a very messy room to be spotless in an hour is a long shot. However, focusing on two or three "surface cleaning" tasks *is* doable. You could pick up dirty clothes and shoes, throw out rumpled scraps of paper, and put away books that are lying around. That would be a really good start. And you could reward yourself afterward with a break. You might even want to relax on your newly cleared floor! (Attaining goals can be very satisfying.)

When you say, *"I'm going to clean my room"* (or the garage, or the kitchen, or the backyard), you are embarking upon a big, and potentially discouraging, undertaking. It may be something to aim for, but by breaking it down into manageable activities in the form of smaller and flexible interim goals that you can actually reach (and feel good about reaching!) it will be easier for you to get things done. You'll be less likely to procrastinate, and more likely to get started, and to finish what you start.

Saying, "*I'm going to clean my room*," or "*I'm going to stop procrastinating about cleaning my room*," is vague. They're broad intentions. You need to be more precise. Try saying, "*I'm going to spend an hour and* 1) *pick up my clothes,* 2) *toss garbage, and* 3) *shelve books.*" That's much more specific and likely to result in success. You have three distinct activities in mind. And, you've given yourself a timeline of one hour.

By selecting and then setting out to do things that are positive and explicit—like picking up, tossing out, and putting stuff in its proper place—you're taking an action-oriented approach toward the goal of tidying up your room. You're also making more of a targeted commitment. You can decide on a manageable time frame. Maybe an hour is too long, or too short to accomplish the three tasks (you may want to start with just one or two tasks), but the grace period is up to you. It's okay if you have to adjust the timing as you go. Take pride in the process, not the speed. For all you know, you may become so inspired that you'll want to tackle a fourth tidying activity—such as sweeping under the bed! One goal can lead to another.

You've probably heard the expression, "*from start to finish.*" Well, how about "*from smart to finish*" instead? Think of the letters in SMART as standing for goals that are Specific, Manageable, Attainable, Realistic, and Timely.[33]

It also helps if you believe a goal is meaningful. Are you going to be cleaning your room for your parents' sake because they're nagging you, or are you going to do it for your own sake? It's useful to reposition your thinking so you're not submitting to someone else's will or demands. Change your outlook to realize that you are accountable; you're developing an action plan *for yourself* with *your own ideas* as to how to reach *your goal*. A room (or desk, or recreation area) can be cluttered, stifling, and smelly—or it can be neat and pleasant. You have a say in making your environment pleasant and motivating, and in making the right choices for your own personal comfort and success. You will benefit. (And, by the way, if you actually prefer to live in the midst of a mess, then that's a conversation you and your parents can have. Some people flourish in chaos. Indeed, goal setting may involve negotiation with others, and perhaps even with yourself.)

The room-cleaning example above is just that—an example. Other goal setting may have to do with your completing school assignments, improving athletic skills, eating less junk food, or something else entirely. The key thing to remember is to be SMART about it, to make sure it matters to you (or else you won't commit to it), and to take that first step.

Here are some other strategies that will help you set workable goals.

. . . .

TIPS for when you procrastinate because of difficulty setting goals

○ **What do you envision?** Picture success. What you want the end result to look like? Perhaps your goal is to finish a science project on volcanoes. Will the final product be a model, chart, poster board, lab report, composition, colored maps illustrating locations of active and dormant volcanoes, or another kind of creative endeavor? Having the format of the goal in mind will help you start the goal-setting process.

○ **Be calm.** When you feel flustered, it's difficult to focus and think clearly, and you have to think clearly in order to set SMART goals. What helps calm you down? Tap into that calming technique when you need it.

○ **Use straightforward wording.** When setting goals, keep your intent and your action plan clear and simple. A goal that is complicated or involves too many steps or detours can be confusing and difficult to manage.

○ **Specify your intended timeline.** Goals that do not have a set timeline might look like this: "*I'll read the chapter at some point later today.*" Or, "*I'll read it when I have a chance.*" It's better to specify a realistic timeline for completion with minimal or no procrastination. It might look like this: "*I'll start as soon as I finish dinner, and read for half an hour.*" Or, "*I'll start reading now and take a break in twenty minutes.*"

○ **What does "as soon as possible" mean?** ASAP is something we see and say a lot. But it has no constraints, and it lets a person off the hook because "soon" could be any time. And, if a task turns out to be impossibly difficult (or complicated, or time-consuming), then it minimizes the possibility of reaching the goal. As a result, "as soon as possible" could mean anything. It's potentially an empty promise.

○ **What's most important now?** When embarking on a project, it may be helpful to deal with the small stuff later. Ask yourself if you can come back to the less important or trivial parts. Plan to prioritize, to focus primarily on the aspects that are most important.

○ **Think about what's worked for you before.** When setting a goal, consider previous goals you've established for yourself, how much time it took you to actually meet them, and what kinds of difficulties, ease, or pleasures you encountered in the process. When you set new goals, keep these guidelines in mind so you can learn from your past experiences.

○ **Is the goal realistic?** Does the goal fit with your capabilities? Is it challenging enough to be interesting, but not so challenging as to be unreachable? What kind of back up support or plan do you have in case you get bogged down? Are there likely to be lots of distractions once you begin, and if so, how can you eliminate them beforehand? Do you have the materials you need? These are questions you can ask yourself so you won't be tempted to procrastinate.

○ **Review your goals.** Be flexible. You might have to adjust your effort, strategies, or timelines part way through a task. For example, if others have similar goals, and you can see how they go about attaining them, or how they overcome problems, you could get useful ideas and then want to revisit your own goals or plans.

○ **Are you willing?** Having a goal is fine, but achieving it will require effort. If you're not going to commit, then is it worth setting the goal? If you're just going to stare (not start), then perhaps the goal is too lofty or unsuitable. Think through it more carefully so you can arrive at a goal that you *are* prepared to try and reach.

○ **Taking a short cut is not necessarily a cop out.** Some goals are reached by means of a long journey, others by a shorter or faster route. How do you want to get to your goal? For example, let's say you're going to cook spaghetti and tomato sauce for your family's dinner. You could do the sauce from scratch, by chopping the tomatoes, onions, garlic, mushrooms, and peppers, cooking it, adding all the seasonings, letting it simmer, and mixing it regularly. Or you could open a jar of prepared chunky tomato sauce and simply heat it up. You might base your decision upon preferences, cost, time factors, additional demands you have to meet, and other considerations, and these may change from day to day. Any way you slice it (no pun intended), you will meet the goal of having spaghetti sauce. How you do that is up to you.

○ **Who can help you reach your goals?** Friends? Family members? Teachers? Mentors or coaches? Who can you count on to encourage and support you? Think about who is available to offer constructive feedback, and help you explore options, find resources, and make sensible and informed decisions when setting goals, and while striving to reach them.

○ **Focus on your own fulfillment.** Your goals are *your* goals. Make them count because you're the one who has to put forth the work that will be required. If someone else is setting the demands or expectations, then figure out why that goal is relevant to you. Why is it worthwhile to do it their way? Or how might you personalize it for your own satisfaction? If a task has meaning and relevance for you, it will help you resolve to start, and to see things through.

• •

Educator Benjamin E. Mays emphasized the importance of having goals. He said, *"It isn't a disgrace not to reach the stars, but it is a disgrace to have no stars to reach for."* Goals help us to learn, and also to grow in new and exciting ways. Reaching a goal is satisfying, and it can be motivating, too. The important thing is this: when you find something you want to aim for or you see the need to do something, set a goal that's achievable, and then take that first step to achieve it.

BUT...Prioritizing and decision-making are hard

We make a great many decisions over the course of the days, weeks, months, and years of our lives. The sum total of these decisions helps to define what we do, and who we are. Sometimes, we decide things quite quickly, whereas other times it takes us longer. Some decisions are hard; some are easy. They can be made independently or with other people. Decisions can have serious, long-term consequences, or little or no impact. Sometimes, we know exactly what we're doing when we make a decision, but sometimes we're unsure and so we just guess or pretend to know, and hope that we're doing the right thing. A decision can take us out of our ordinary comfort zones, and into unfamiliar areas. Decisions can be silly, unyielding, life-or-death, flexible, precise, thoughtful, joyful, regretful, big, small, hesitant, right, wrong, and so on...However, we can't escape decision-making because our lives are full of choices every day. (Decision-making is really important—so much so that it's the focus of the very first endnote in this book. You'll see information on the stages of decision-making in that endnote.)

The best decision is an informed one. Facts and knowledge steer us in the right directions. They help us to know what to pay attention to first—that is, how to prioritize. Once we have solid foundational information, we're better prepared to move forward. Which means we're less likely to procrastinate.

Where do people acquire the kinds of information that will be useful to them? How do people prioritize things? How do decision-makers go about making good decisions? Here are some answers to these questions, along with suggestions, too.

• •

TIPS for when you procrastinate because of difficulty prioritizing and decision-making

○ **Information is everywhere.** Before you make a decision, think about what you need to know in order to arrive at a wise choice. People, places, and things are all potential sources of valuable information. Listen. Talk. Observe. Read. The time you spend acquiring current and dependable information is time well spent. If you put off doing something because you're trying to find out more so you can prioritize or arrive at a decision, you may not be procrastinating. Think of it as directing your energy productively. Once you've done that, however, move on.

○ **Reflect.** It's good to be thoughtful when making decisions. As in the example above, the time you spend doing this is not procrastinating. You might call it a careful and deliberate strategy. Reflection is worthwhile because it will help you to clarify and consolidate ideas, and also to explore your options, attitudes, and assumptions. However, don't overdo the reflective aspect to the point where you neglect actually starting whatever it is you're busy thinking about. Saying that you're thinking really hard about how to go about writing a book report is fine, as long as you also resolve to set aside enough time to write it. Ideally before it's due.

○ **Decisions can also be changed.** Sometimes decisions are made, and then afterward you want to alter them. This happens to people all the time. We decide to change clothes, schools, music, and other aspects of our lives. And, why not? Do you procrastinate just because you think your decision about how to approach something might end up being wrong? Give it a shot. You can fix errors and learn from mistakes. However, if you decide to do nothing or to procrastinate, you're at a standstill. Ancient Greek poet Sophocles wrote these wise words, *"Fortune cannot aid those who do nothing."*

○ **On the other hand…** Another ancient Greek, the physician Hippocrates, said, *"To do nothing is also a good remedy."* Hmmm. This also bears thinking about; after all, Hippocrates (who is often referred to as the father of medicine) was no slouch! Doing nothing may be okay in some situations—like not responding to an insult, or not disturbing a nest outside your bedroom window even though the birds are chirping and waking you at the crack of dawn. But Hippocrates' advice does not apply to everything we have to deal with, or else how would anything ever get done?

○ **Juggling priorities can be tricky.** Schedules are increasingly jam-packed, filled with commitments, activities, and challenges. It's not easy to balance all, or even some of this. Sometimes it's hard to get to everything. You may experience delays, forward bursts, or backward slides, even though you hope to make steady progress.[34] You may have trouble knowing what to address first, then next, and next…You might, for example, consider going on the basis of what seems most urgent (that is, needs immediate attention), or might have the most serious consequences if you don't follow through. If you have several assignments to do and you aren't sure which one you should tackle first, think about which might have flexible due dates, and which ones involve other people who are counting on you. Which assignment will probably take more (or less) time for you to complete? Think it through, and plan accordingly.

○ **Share the burden.** We regularly share experiences, feelings, ideas, and opinions with others, so it's not unreasonable to share decision-making as well. It's best to do this with people who care, and whose input you think will be helpful. Communication is the key. Moreover, there's so much technology at our fingertips that collaborative effort is easier than ever. Sharing a load can help forge relationships, broaden viewpoints, lessen risks, strengthen decisions—and all of this can begin with a conversation or a few taps of a keyboard.

○ **Decisions take me too long.** Sometimes people take a loooong time to decide how to prioritize things and how, or even if, they should do something because they're afraid that if the outcome is bad, they'll lose control, or get into trouble, or others will think less of them. All of that is understandable. If you feel this way (that is, hesitant and unsure), perhaps ask yourself, *"What's the absolute worst that could happen?"* and then figure out a couple of ways you might deal with that scenario.[35] Realistically, chances are "the absolute worst" won't happen, so you'll be able to manage anything less. You may not want to move too fast, but don't let that stop you from moving at all. Think of a car sitting at an intersection. Once the light turns green, how long can the car just stay there? It has to go sooner or later. It might as well be sooner.

• •

Decisions are forerunners to change. These can be unfamiliar, upsetting, or scary, which is why some people put off or avoid decisions that could lead to change. Try to anticipate what will lie ahead as a result of making a decision; in that way, you can plan a sensible course of action. When you know you have strategies for dealing with change, you'll feel more prepared, relaxed, and confident, and therefore less likely to procrastinate.

BUT...I don't have the knowledge

The future is unknown. We can't predict what will happen. However, we will have more knowledge tomorrow than we do today because we'll have more experiences to draw upon. Knowledge builds over time through opportunities to experience the world and to learn.

Saying you don't want to do something because you don't have the knowledge is a common way of thinking. Yet, if that lack or deficiency is causing you to procrastinate, or perhaps even stopping you in your tracks, how can you go about getting the knowledge you require?

The answer lies in moving forward, not in stalling, procrastinating, or avoiding things. Try to be as open as possible to whatever knowledge comes along, using that to inform your thoughts and actions. It helps if you *ask* intelligent questions, *listen* carefully to the answers, and then *think* about them. Tap your senses; sight, sound, touch, taste, feel, and smell. They can provide you with fresh insights. Consider new ways of looking at things. Study what's around you, and then look beyond. Knowledge comes in different forms and from different sources. It accumulates incrementally (that is, step by step, piece by piece), and this accumulation can occur not only when and where you expect it (like at school), but also when and where you don't expect it (like when you're out for a walk and you suddenly encounter someone or something interesting or brand new). Be adventurous. If you're not sure about what lies ahead, you can take some time to assess the risks, plan precautions, get the support you need, and decide if you want to proceed cautiously or just stay put. Which brings us right back to the decision-making considerations in the previous section!

Here are some more thoughts and tips having to do with procrastinators who let insufficient knowledge get in the way of progress.

TIPS for when you procrastinate because of a lack of knowledge

○ **Start with what you know.** Use what you know and what you can do as building blocks for more know-how. It will give you confidence.

○ **Stretch in new and unexpected ways.** Extend your capabilities. Discovery and curiosity will pave the way for creative ventures. Embracing your creativity (rather than worrying about the difficulty of a task) can motivate you! Here are three strategies to get your creative juices flowing: 1) Determine what excites you, what makes you feel good about yourself, and what gives you a "spring in your step." 2) Spend some time thinking about creative possibilities and how to make them happen. 3) Readjust your thinking about your abilities and what you *can* do!

○ **"I don't know" is a common phrase.** It's not the same as saying, "*I can't*," or "*I'm stupid*," or "*There's no point in doing this*." However, it is the same as saying, "*This is an opportunity for me to learn*." Reassure yourself that you know a lot, and with effort and possibly some help, you can do the task.

○ **All knowledge starts somewhere.** "*Perplexity is the beginning of knowledge*." Poet Kahlil Gibran said this, and the message, as I see it, is that you shouldn't be ashamed or apologetic about not knowing stuff, or think that you have to understand everything around you. Realistically, there's more we *don't* know than we *do* know, so don't be too hard on yourself for being at "the beginning of knowledge," or let that cause you to limit your actions.

○ **Find someone who knows what you don't.** Who can help you learn what you want or need to know? A friend? A mentor? An advisor? You might even be gracious and offer an exchange of knowledge with someone who can help you out.

○ **Think ahead.** Imagine looking into the future a bit. Think about how great you'll feel once you make the effort to discover what you need to know to get started on what you have to do. You'll not only feel good, you'll feel excited and empowered.

• •

There are many forms of knowledge. Have faith in what you already know—and all that you're able to learn. Get started!

BUT...hey, look at my track record (past experience)

You probably know yourself better than anyone else does. And, every kind of ability that you've acquired over the years was developed step by step over time. You have a sense of what you're good at, what takes more time or practice, what you enjoy, and what you dislike. All of this is based on your past experiences, and on what you've learned from these experiences.

If you're asked to do something that's familiar, you can probably guess how much time or work you'll need. You can think about how you tackled similar tasks in the past, and then plan accordingly. For example, if it took you five days to research and write your last book report, and you did well on it, chances are you'll need five days in order to complete the next report. You can safely put it off until then.

However, what if the next report is more complicated or detailed? Or the book is more difficult? Or the research is more demanding? Or the assessment is more complex? Or you require a different skill set? Then you might need longer than five days to complete the work. Your track record is a good way to estimate how much time you may need, but realistically you also have to take into account other factors that could have a bearing on that time frame. There is always the "unknown" element, something unexpected, that could interfere with your plan. For instance, what if you get the flu, or another big assignment comes along, or you need extra help, or there's a family situation that requires your attention? If you've left yourself only a limited amount of time to complete the book report, then you may find yourself scrambling, and you may not be able get it done. How would you feel then?

Past experience and track records are useful guidelines. Procrastinating based on those guidelines can make sense—to a point. You could end up having to rush toward completion if you wait too long to get started. And, you may be able to do a better job if you allow yourself a longer time frame. Try to make wise decisions. Be mindful of your skills and previous accomplishments, and take pride in the effort you put forth. Build on your record of previous successes; you've earned that right! Be sure to give yourself some leeway when planning what you have to do the next time around. Life sometimes has a way of fooling us, and it's better to have a little extra time than to run out of it.

Here are some planning tips—ways to base what you have to do on past experience or your record of accomplishments, while not being overly dependent on them.

- -

TIPS for when you procrastinate based on your past experience

○ **Use an agenda or calendar.** Mark things down so you're aware of what you have to complete, and when. This will help you now, and also in the future (when you want to refer back to what you've done). Check your agenda to see what you did, and maybe even how long it took you last time.

○ **Plan smart.** When's the task due? Be certain. Is there any flexibility? Once you know, work out how much time you think you'll need to complete it. Lots of teens find it's helpful to work that out backwards from when something has to be done. Be generous by adding in some extra time for good measure. Use that agenda—or another "planning sheet" to record the steps you plan to take.

○ **What are your areas of strength and weakness?** If there are particular aspects of the task that you expect will be easy, you can plan to devote less time to those, leaving more time to spend on whatever might be difficult. Think back to what you've experienced before, paying attention to ease and difficulty. Then think ahead, and apply this knowledge. (Remember, if you want to add something especially creative or different, you may need to budget extra time for that.)

○ **Are you easily distracted?** What has diverted your attention before, causing you to procrastinate? Take those possible distractions into account.

○ **Alone or with others?** If others are involved in a task you have to do, can you count on them to do their part? (How do you know? Perhaps you have some idea about that based on having worked with them before.) You might need to plan for "contingency" time—that is, extra, in case there's an unforeseen incident, lag, or problem.

○ **Are you impulsive?** If you know that you sometimes suddenly get great ideas, consider what you might do about that. When something arises that isn't part of your plan, write it down and save it for later. Unless you can see a way to slot it in right away, it makes more sense to stick to what you have to do first and foremost. Remain focused on one set goal at a time, broken down into steps and manageable intervals from beginning to end.

○ **Trust your instincts.** If, based on past experience, you think you'll need a week to accomplish something, give yourself a week. Then be kind to yourself and add bonus time in case you encounter any setbacks. If you don't need that bonus time, it will be there and you can use it for something you really enjoy doing. It will give you an incentive to get started, and to reach your goal faster.

○ **Check off steps as you proceed.** Seeing steps checked off on an agenda or planning sheet is a good way to monitor your progress, and determine if you're on track. For example, electronic trackers like Fitbit encourage people to develop good habits and keep active by recording steps, and these devices also regularly send congratulatory messages and morale boosters. The huge popularity of these personal trackers attests to the motivational impact of self-monitoring. (*"Ten thousand steps? Hey, I did that!"*) Similarly, a visual action plan or agenda can encourage you to move forward. It's also like a road map because it makes it easier to picture your upcoming steps, and stick to them, or possibly revise them, if need be. (It's also handy to refer back to.) And, you'll feel upbeat and more confident when you see the "tracked" results or check marks indicating what you've accomplished!

○ **Recall.** Think about times when you procrastinated in the past. What happened? How did you handle the situations? What can you learn from that? What do you think you might do differently next time? A word of caution: sometimes recollections are faulty. Are your memories and interpretations of past events (including the extent of the demands, and timelines) correct? They may merit closer reflection to make sure.

• •

Past experience is a form of history, and history helps to inform the present and the future. However, try not to get trapped, or to be too strongly influenced by what you've done or what's happened before. Rather, use your past experiences (your own personal history) as a sort of guideline, warning system, or illuminating beam to help you proceed. The past can give you some direction as you chart a course of action today, and stride more confidently toward tomorrow.

BUT...I have difficulty with time management (and planning and preparation)

United States President John F. Kennedy said, *"We must use time as a tool, not as a couch."* And, Israeli Prime Minister Golda Meir said, *"I must govern the clock, not be governed by it."*

These two former leaders of nations understood that time is valuable. Time is an asset we all have. Yet how we use it makes a huge difference in how we define and arrange to reach goals, what we accomplish, or if we even get in motion at all.

Adults and kids often find it tricky to manage time, so if you do, too, you're not alone! When thinking about what has to be done, remember that planning it out, or even preparing to do it, is not the same as actually doing it. You may have trouble getting started, or you may encounter situations you didn't expect along the way. You may have difficulty concentrating. You may require additional or different resources. You may discover that you need more time than you thought. You may procrastinate.

Managing time is a skill that has to be learned. Ideally, this begins in childhood. Unfortunately, many children don't receive those kinds of lessons in daily practice.

For example, perhaps your parents asked—and still ask—questions like, *"Have you started your homework?"* *"Are you doing your homework now?"* *"Have you finished your homework yet?"* They're overseeing the process, but they're also essentially managing your life for you. They're basically laying down ground rules, indicating that you ought to do this, that they expect you to do that—and when. Some parents wake teens up in the morning, and then schedule and orchestrate their "getting ready for school" routines so they won't be late. Other parents set out expectations for after school hours, or for evenings.

This kind of scheduling may help the household run smoothly on a daily basis, and for many families a set regimen like this works well. However, many teens find it difficult to adhere to strict or predetermined parameters, and would rather develop their own, with more flexible timelines and deadlines. Autonomy becomes increasingly important as kids get older.

It's good to have routines in place. With that said, parents who take *too* much control of homework or daily activities may not be doing their kids any favors because they will miss out on opportunities to learn how to manage their time effectively and independently.

When parents encourage teens to be accountable for their homework and timeliness—and then back off or step aside—teens either get things done, or they don't. If homework is incomplete, or if they are repeatedly late for school, they will have to deal with the consequences. Consequences provide a learning curve. Young people who take matters into their own hands, and resolve to become responsible and to use time wisely, begin to appreciate the value of structure, and of developing responsibility.

So, if you're concerned about your time management skills, resolve to take charge and strengthen them. Instead of relying on your parents or others to set schedules for you, consider how you can schedule yourself. Rather than having other people show or tell you what to do with your time, figure it out on your own (or possibly with adults' assistance until you get things in place). Then move forward, and take pride in that. In fact, you might want to support and encourage others as they struggle to manage their time effectively, too.

There are many strategies people use to develop stronger time management skills.[36] Some are general, and based on common sense. Others are more specific, or depend on the particular situation. Here are some time management suggestions that are particularly useful for procrastinators. I've also included some tips relating to planning and preparation because, quite frankly, they can take up a lot of time. You can increase your productivity if you learn to be efficient.

. . . .

TIPS for when you procrastinate because of difficulty with time management (and planning and preparation)

○ **It's about attitude.** Start by being willing to take the steps you need to be in control of your time. Work out how long you think it will take to do your homework, or to complete your morning routine, or whatever else you have to do, and make up your mind that you're not going to let someone else set the pace. You can and will be in charge.

○ **Do you need help?** Identify who can give you some assistance in learning how to create workable schedules.

○ **Allot time for each aspect of a task.** What does a fair timeline look like for the sort of task you have to complete? Break the task down into manageable segments, and plan how much time you will need for each, blocking it off so you can see it. Be sure to think about possible setbacks. If you have a clear sense of how you intend to use your time, and it seems fair and doable, you'll be more likely to get started and less likely to procrastinate.

○ **Stick with it.** If you go off track, you will require more time. If people or things distract you, or you get busy with "other stuff," it's important to try and regain focus on whatever it is you need to do. (For more on distractions, see the first section in Chapter 4.)

○ **Count on routine.** Tasks and chores that are commonplace can also become automatic or routine, and there's a certain amount of comfort in that. Although recurring activities or duties still require commitment, the familiarity can help you plan and prepare. For example, you can leave out your clothes the night before for quick access in the morning, and keep your breakfast options easy. The less complicated the routine, the better.

○ **You can say, "No thanks."** There are only 24 hours in a day, and if you try to do everything you want to do, you may run the risk of losing sight of what's most important. It may be better—and certainly more honest—to prioritize and as a result admit that you won't do something, rather than to say that you will do it and then dither, procrastinate, or not see it through. You may think saying "*yes*" instead of "*no*" will set you on a deliberate path going forward, and that you will be able to manage (the task, the timing required, the obstacles, and so on). It's possible. However, meeting a challenge requires preparation, effort, pacing, and time— and sometimes a polite *"no thanks"* (or even a *"maybe later"* but only IF you're up for it), will enable you to manage your 24 hours and your own priorities more effectively.[37]

○ **Is looking back a waste of time?** It's useful to reflect on previous experience, and it's good to see (and gain confidence from) how far you've come. After all, learning builds from what you already know.[38] That said, spending too much time dwelling on the past (what has already happened), may not be as productive as focusing on the future (what is yet to be). Be purposeful. Face forward. Move forward.

○ **Value time, and use surprise snippets well.** Time is valuable. Sometimes it seems to vanish, but occasionally you find extra! For example, if a sports practice or music session gets cancelled, you may suddenly have time to spare. A fifteen-minute interval can be like a welcome flash of light. Moreover, it's manageable. Get in the habit of using short blocks of "free" time to get things done. You could de-clutter a drawer, answer messages, help a friend, or exercise. Even a couple of minutes can be bonus time.

○ **Try using a timer.** It's a very basic approach but it can work. There are interesting timers available, including electronic gadgets, apps, and colorful sand-filled glass containers. Set the device for a certain amount of time. Begin, and stick with what you're doing until the timer runs down. Then take a break, and reset it. Think of this like a game; you're competing against the clock, while also accomplishing things. Another advantage: games help fuel creativity, and vice versa.

○ **Will technology save the day?** Technology may simplify many aspects of life, but devices do not necessarily translate into more time. The world is fast-paced, and even if we multi-task, there seems to be more to do than ever. Technology programs promise to make us more efficient and organized—Todolist, Evernote, and Google Calendar are just three tools out of hundreds.[39] But beware. People often believe they're gaining time, but end up tinkering, or possibly working faster but not necessarily smarter. Also, sometimes people choose programs that are unnecessarily elaborate and wind up wasting precious time figuring out the intricacies instead of doing what they have to do.

○ **Spur of the moment is also okay.** You can try being spontaneous. That is, seize the moment, improvise, go without a carefully designed plan, and just see what happens. For example, many wonderful comedy routines and musical jam sessions are unrehearsed and created without any preplanning. Lots of great travel experiences are makeshift or impromptu. It may be a bit risky to do something "on the fly" but you might be happily surprised. (This is not an "always" suggestion. For the most part, planning and preparation are still important and yield better results for most people.)

○ **Adjust as you go.** Tennis players adjust the way they twist, turn, lunge, and reach, depending on which way the tennis ball flies. They have to be prepared to react to each serve and volley. Life is not a tennis competition, but it is full of unexpected occurrences, including interruptions, changes, and distractions. Plan to use time wisely, but stay flexible in case things get tricky.

• •

Time management makes it easier to get into action mode. And, action is a means to overcome procrastination. In the words of ancient Roman poet, Virgil, *"Time is flying, never to return."* It's better to learn to take advantage of time than to let it slip through your fingers. (If you want additional resources and strategies for time management, check out the segment in Chapter 5.)

BUT...I'd rather do something else instead

Task substitution involves doing one thing when you're supposed to be doing another. For example, let's say you're supposed to be straightening out your closet, and instead you decide to tidy up your desk drawer. You're still straightening stuff, but you've changed your focus. Are you procrastinating?

Yes. You might not think so, but you are. That's because you're choosing to put something off.

There are many reasons why people might choose to do one thing rather than another, postponing or avoiding a task or demand (X), and focusing on a different one instead (Y). For example, X may be more exciting, challenging, easier, urgent, or enjoyable than Y (as in Yucky). Teens are often tempted to procrastinate when asked to do tasks that seem unappealing (like having to brush knots out of the dog's fur), or scary (like having to clean up an area of the basement when they're convinced there may be spiders lurking there), or too difficult (like studying for a comprehensive test), or time consuming (like having to write a pile of thank you notes on the weekend when you have people to see and places to go).

Most teens want to appear capable and well intentioned. They may not admit or even recognize that they're procrastinating. After all, they're doing "another" activity, and that makes them believe they're accomplishing something. Moreover, busyness is a way to show others, and also to convince themselves, that they aren't lazy or putting things off. However, sometimes busyness gets bigger and bigger, and it interferes with getting things done. And, at the end of the day (or week), the seemingly Yucky task still awaits... (By the way, since yuckiness is a matter of perception, you might consider whether you're exaggerating the negativity. Even a mud puddle can be a beautiful thing if you want to splash around in the rain and don't care about getting filthy).

There are things you can do to redirect your attention to what really needs to be started—and completed—and also stay focused.

. . . .

TIPS for when you procrastinate because you'd rather do other things

○ **Make it fun.** Have to do something boring or unpleasant? Sing or dance along to music, make the activity into a game. Get together with friends and create an innovative and enjoyable way to get the job done. Try and be creative.

○ **Respect your own preferences.** If you really can't stand the idea of doing something, talk to someone you trust about this. Maybe there are ways to get around it, pass some of it over to someone else, or approach it gradually so it's not quite as unappealing, scary, difficult, or time consuming. Think about the possibilities. Polite refusal is an option, but it has to be a *reasoned* one—negotiated, sensible, and considerate.

○ **Divide and conquer.** If you want to postpone a task and do something else, then make an effort to keep that something else to a minimum. Spend some time (but not too much) on the preferred activity, and then move on to the less preferred one. You can go back and forth between the two. It would be helpful to schedule time for both.

○ **Delegate.** Sometimes it makes sense to let someone else take over a good chunk of what you have to do, so you have more time to accomplish what you really need or want to do. You might not be able to get to everything, and delegating is a way of getting help and relieving the pressure of having to deal with too much, or with something that's upsetting to you.

○ **Just do it.** It's a popular advertising slogan. It's possibly not exactly what you want to see or hear as a "strategy" right here. Nevertheless, it's how you should think if you're going to get a nasty or challenging task done. Take a deep breath, stop doing whatever is getting in the way, and resolve to "*just do it.*"

○ **Ask yourself…Is the task as awful as you think?** Things you believe are disgusting may not be so bad once you give them a try. For example, slimy fish may sound awful, but sushi could be delicious. And rubber gloves and nose plugs can make even disgusting tasks almost bearable.

○ **Trade off.** What you find Yucky may actually be something someone else doesn't mind doing. Offer to exchange jobs. If they're willing to clean the fish tank (or rake the lawn, or scrape the layers of ice off the porch steps, or bathe the dog), make a deal. They can take over for you. And, you can arrange to do something for them—something that you like better. As a bonus, you'll probably be able to get through that more quickly if it's not as offensive, thus giving you even more time to do what you enjoy doing.

○ **Think when…then!** Make a deal with yourself. *When* you get to a certain point, *then* you can take some time to do what you'd prefer to do.

○ **Approach with interest.** Try to readjust your viewpoint. Instead of avoiding or putting off a potentially displeasing experience, think of the task as interesting, and as a chance to stretch yourself, and overcome an aversion.

• •

Life is a mix of pleasant and unpleasant experiences. Recognizing that you will inevitably encounter both might help you strive to find a happy balance so that you can move ahead without procrastinating. William Shakespeare wrote, *"There is nothing either good or bad but thinking makes it so."*[40] Don't put constraints on yourself by your thinking. If you do what you don't want to do, you may find having done it is truly—and perhaps surprisingly—worthwhile.

BUT…I hate doing anything that's risky

Risk implies danger, and danger is something we typically try to avoid. Rightly so!

However, risk and danger come in different shapes and sizes. There's playful "rough and tumble" type risky behavior (which is not so bad). And then there's full jolt "injury" type behavior (which is far more dangerous). Be smart. Danger is not always obvious. On the other hand, risk can seem bigger than it really is. Figuring out the difference between low-risk and high-risk situations will help you understand whether to sidestep or avoid something, or possibly go ahead with it. An adult or trustworthy friend can assist you if you're not sure.

There's good reason to procrastinate or to refuse to do things that could threaten your health, safety, or well-being. However, if a task or activity is just a bit dicey, unpredictable, or chancy, then it may not be such a big deal. Also, some people have lots of gumption, whereas others are more timid. Ancient Roman historian Sallust said, *"Necessity makes even the timid brave."* In other words, if you *have* to do something or it's important to you, there's a greater likelihood that you will summon up courage and strive to overcome any apparent risk. However, if the task or activity is not required, or it's just a whim, you may be tempted to procrastinate.

When facing a potentially perilous situation, it helps to know what you're capable of doing. For example, if you've never been in a kayak, and you aren't familiar with how to get on board, paddle, or stay balanced, you might decide to procrastinate rather than going kayaking—especially on your own. It could be risky. However, if you have a friend who can show you how to manage the boat, and patiently help you learn to paddle and maintain balance, then there is less risk involved. The more knowledge and skills you acquire, the lower the risk. Start at the shore or riverbank in just a few inches of water while learning the basics. And, remember to always wear a personal flotation device (PFD) for added safety!

Here are more ways to lessen risk, and the tendency to procrastinate because of it.

TIPS for when you procrastinate because a task is risky

○ **Gauge the extent of the risk.** Is it really as risky as you think it is? How can you be sure? What is the evidence? Is there some way to make it less risky? Is there someone you can ask? Figure out how big the risk is before getting too worked up about it.

○ **Inspirational words can give you courage.** There's an endless supply of motivational quotes that might help you get through challenging situations. Whether it's a risk, a difficulty, a hazard, or a hoax, the wise words of others can pave the way for you to move forward with greater resolve. Investigate the words of someone whose judgments or deeds you admire. For example, here's a quote from Mark Zuckerberg (Internet entrepreneur, and co-founder of Facebook): *"The biggest risk is not taking any risk...In a world that's changing really quickly, the only strategy that is guaranteed to fail is not taking risks."* Words to think about![41]

○ **Skirt around the risk.** You may be putting something off because it's risky, but it may only be partly so. Can you divide the task into the more and less risky aspects? If so, you can start on the parts that are most comfortable for you. This could give you confidence to keep going, even if it becomes tricky.

○ **Find the change agent.** What will it take to make the task less risky? If something is hot, try ice cubes. If it's too dark, get a flashlight. If it's mysterious or unknown, find out more about it. There's usually some way to moderate the risk. Get creative. Be resourceful.

○ **Risk is not all bad.** There can be an upside to confronting risk. Provided you don't endanger yourself, there's often a learning curve and also a sense of triumph upon overcoming a seemingly precarious or challenging situation. For example, let's say you're putting off learning how to skate because you think that you'll fall on the ice and hurt yourself. Skating may seem risky to you. However, if you take it really slow, skate with someone else, wear the right equipment, and keep practicing, the danger you perceive will decrease. Pace yourself, be smart about tackling a risk, and chances are you will succeed.

○ **Let someone else take the lead.** Do you know anyone who is more capable of tackling the particular task, and who will therefore find it less risky? (Using the example above, perhaps someone who is a good skater who can guide you as you learn to skate.) If this person takes the first steps, or is willing to share the load, you may not feel the need to procrastinate.

○ **Who enjoys risk?** Some people like to experiment (or bungee-jump, or try to walk a tight-rope)—or take risks. If you know someone like that, talk to them and discover why. You can also get advice from them as to how they might have overcome being fearful of any risk. People who make an effort to learn from the lived experience of others often find they begin to worry less, and may even see some risks as not-so-scary after all.

○ **Prepare for possible outcomes.** If you know what to expect, you can ready yourself for the consequences of your actions, manage the results, and be brave even if it's a risky situation. Businessman Warren Buffet said, "*Risk comes from not knowing what you're doing.*" So, with that in mind, get busy and start knowing! Think ahead to make sure you have what you'll need if the risky situation you're avoiding does become difficult. (Think back to the kayaking or ice skating examples above. If you were to fall in the water or fall down on the ice, what would make it bearable? What would you wish to have? Who could possibly help?) Be prepared for challenge but hope for the best. Concentrate on the process and on the result, not on the risk.

• •

Life is full of risks. Changing schools. Meeting new people. Leaving home for a summer at overnight camp or a year at college. Singing or speaking in front of an audience. Anything that's worth doing may involve some degree of risk. However, the only way you'll know how much you can accomplish is if you try. You can push yourself and go places and do things—or you can sit still or stand around and do the bare minimum.

Be positive! For example, change the thought of "risk" to "adventure" or "escapade" or "opportunity" instead. Take what's sometimes called "a calculated risk" by thinking about the likelihood that you will prevail if you have courage, use your know-how, and put forth effort. Hesitation and procrastination only delay action. If necessary, reduce the risk, and resolve to rise above it. Build your wings, find your strength, and take pride in your ability. You can do it. Life has its share of deterrents. Rise above them!

Chapter 4

External Reasons for Procrastination: What Are Your BUTS?

Jiminy Cricket: "Now you see, the world is full of temptations."

Pinocchio: "Temptations?"

Jiminy Cricket: "Yep, temptations. They're the wrong things that seem right at the time."

BUT...I get distracted

Distractions—what are they? Songs; gadgets; Instagram; a comment made by someone nearby; golden sunsets; a puppy; or...? We can easily be distracted by these things—and more. However, we also have the ability to put our minds to the task at hand, even though tuning out music, electronic devices, words, beauty, cute animals, and so forth can be difficult.

Sometimes we begin a task and stay on course, and other times we get sidelined. This may be unintentional (we want to move forward, but the distraction is just too strong), or it may be deliberate (we focus on the distraction because it's more interesting or fun). Distractions may be big, little, tasty, smelly, noisy, or unexpected. They can happen any time. We may not be able to control them.

And they may be unavoidable. (Like hurricanes, power failures, or accidents.)

It just so happens that as I write this, my right leg is swollen and elevated. I'm in pain. I broke my ankle a couple of days ago, and the doctor instructed me to stay off my feet. I'm sitting on the sofa with my computer on my lap. The discomfort is a distraction. I could simply procrastinate and not write. I could say to myself, *"I'm not feeling up to it now."* But the truth is, I can manage the pain, and writing helps take my mind off my injury. If I were to procrastinate, the only person I'd be fooling would be myself. And to what end? Better to continue writing, and to be honest with myself.

When it comes to distractions, it helps to know yourself. That is, what triggers your lack of focus? What can you tolerate or ignore so you stay on track? It's interesting that some people work well with the television on, or with music blaring in the background. Others can't function that way. They're too distracted by the commotion. There are people who are oblivious to doorbells, ringing phones, buzzers, car alarms, and barking dogs, and others who run immediately to see what's going on, and thus become distracted.

When distractions become excuses, or they underlie procrastination, then it may be time to think about finding ways to manage or eliminate them.

- -

TIPS for when you procrastinate because of distractions

○ **What commands your attention?** Make a list of the kinds of things or activities that can distract you and take up valuable time. For example, snacks, texts, games…Is there some way to schedule these in so that you can still enjoy them but so that they won't interfere with your commitments?[42]

○ **Doubts can be distracting.** Lacking confidence in your ability, or being unsure about how to proceed with something, can be distracting. As a result, you may procrastinate. So, ask for help. Ask questions. Ask yourself what you need to feel better about moving forward. Ask whatever you need to ask, until you get answers that satisfy you. Once you get rid of doubts or negativity you will feel better and be more productive.

○ **Remove temptation.** Remove or discard what's likely to disturb you. There's a sensible old saying, *"Out of sight, out of mind."* Put away the potato chips. Turn off the television. Silence your cell phone. Close the window.

○ **Linger for a bit with the distraction—then let it go.** It's okay to stay with the distraction a little, and then carry on purposefully. A distraction can be like a brief break. It doesn't have to take over. Be a "visitor," then depart.

○ **Embrace the many joys of life.** You don't have to apologize for having many interests. Enjoy them. Distractions like music, art, or ice cream sundaes can be fun, and they can make you happy and optimistic. Just remember to use that positive energy as a motivator.

○ **Check the frequency.** How often are you distracted? And why? Keep track of the number of times you're sidetracked over a week or so. It will help you become more aware of what the distractions are, and how they affect your behavior. If you're distracted a LOT, and if it seriously interferes with your productivity, whether at home or at school, then you may have problems with attention. Speak to your parents or teachers if this is an ongoing concern. You may also benefit from acquiring some professional advice.

○ **Train yourself to stay focused.** There are ways you can become more aware of your actions and regulate them. You can learn to prevent yourself from doing things, including being distracted, by working out a system to help keep your behavior in check. For example, you could make a pile of 50 chocolate chips, or raisins, or mini-marshmallows, and whenever you catch yourself being distracted, you remove one and then move on. (You have to resolve to be honest.)

At the end of the day, you get to eat what's left. The less distractions you allow, the more treats you'll enjoy.[43]

○ **Practice mindfulness.** Mindfulness has to do with aware-ness of—and staying in—the moment. This practice of paying attention and not letting the mind wander is being taught in schools all over the world. Mindfulness helps people learn to clear their heads, turn away from distrac-tions, and appreciate the here-and-now. It can also help with mood, productivity, attitude, and overall health. You can find out more about the many benefits of mindfulness elsewhere.[44]

○ **What does current research tell us?** For more incentives on how to curb distractions, increase the desire to take action, and overcome procrastination, check out the podcasts and publications at www.procrastination.ca. You will find information, links, and research-based understandings, offered by the Procrastination Research Group at Carlton University in Canada.

• •

Distractions are natural and inevitable. You have many, many experiences over the course of every day. The nature, duration, and direction of your attention is always changing from one thing to another. If distractions have a negative effect on your well-being or productivity (for example, if they make you upset, unfocused, late, uncooperative, or cause you to procrastinate), then it's time to think about disciplining yourself and getting rid of whatever is causing the interference. The strategies listed in the next section, which deal with structure, may enhance the ones listed above.

BUT...I need more structure

Guidelines and structure can help you understand, and then do, what you have to do, whereas vague expectations make it dif-ficult to pin down what's required—and when. If something is not clear or well defined, that may be reason enough to push it aside.

What's the rush? The need? The reason for tackling it? Why not wait till you're ready or you're in the mood? Or you see the point? Or you have nothing better to do...?

If there's no specific framework, or timeline, or clarity, you may not have to do it now. You can procrastinate. Right?

The truth is, that without parameters (think boundaries), people tend to wander. For example, if you gaze at the entire night sky filled with a zillion stars, your eyes will go every which way, and it will be difficult to concentrate for long on one small cluster. However, if you discipline yourself to focus on just one segment of the vast sky, then you can better appreciate that small constellation. Similarly, if you have a pile of things you have to do, but you don't have a framework for action, then you may be inclined to be all over the place.

When one or more of the tasks that you're supposed to be focused on seem unstructured, unwieldy, or unmanageable, you might put them off. You might not know how to begin, or fully realize what could happen if you don't stick with it. You might decide to avoid the demands entirely, and do something else instead.

Perhaps you think limits and discipline are constricting. *("Be home in an hour." "Do your homework before you go out." "Don't ski down that hill." "Stay with your little brother.")* It may seem as though "requests" like these control your life. However, without boundaries, structures, and rules, the world would be a chaotic mess. If there were no stop signs, traffic lights, and crosswalks, pedestrians and cars would all surge forward at once, and there would be accidents. If there were no food regulations, people would eat unhealthy products and possibly get sick. If there were no timetables and schedules, no one would know when to show up for school or work, or when to catch the bus.

Structure, routines, past experiences, and rules are useful. Once you've done a research paper, you'll know how to do another. Once you've performed in a track meet or a piano recital, you'll know how to prepare for the next one. Rules and past experiences offer a framework of stability. They act as guidelines for proceeding, and for developing self-discipline. They enable people to know what is expected of them so that they have a clear idea of what to do, including how much time they'll need and if, or how much, they can safely veer off course.

It's also important to become aware of the possible consequences of what you choose to do or not do. Thinking about consequences can provide some degree of structure because they indicate the potential outcomes and impact of decisions and choices. What will happen as a result of doing something? Of not doing it? Or procrastinating? You can choose to do as you please (and when you please) but it helps to have a sense of the consequences you might have to face. You probably know the song about the little spider that goes up the waterspout. The spider will get washed out—if it rains. Should it wait? Should it go elsewhere? Should it take its chances? Unknown and unstructured circumstances can be daunting and confusing.

Procrastinators have to use judgment with respect to the particular situation. They should reflect on the structure they have to stick to, and why. Whether it has to do with homework, studying for an exam, or practicing a musical instrument, what's sensible? What will happen if they put off the task? Who will be affected, and how? If there are NO implications or consequences, then procrastinating seems doable. Maybe even acceptable. Otherwise, they should probably get cracking.

Here are some thoughts around how to develop structure and self-discipline, and why this matters when it comes to building momentum and being productive.

• •

TIPS for when you procrastinate because of lack of structure

○ **Self-discipline is important.** In the big scheme of things, you are your own boss. You can be responsible or irresponsible. However, being responsible is harder when the rules are lax, or the boundaries are wishy-washy. Steer yourself well, and use self-discipline as your compass. U. S. President Theodore Roosevelt said, *"With self-discipline,* *most anything is possible."* Remember, you are at the controls; you are the pilot, and pilots have discipline.

○ **Who can inspire you to become more disciplined?**
Dancers? Athletes? Scientists? These role models recognize the value of structure and order. They understand the connections between what they choose to do, and what they ultimately accomplish. They strive and succeed. Can they inspire you?

○ **Structure comes in different forms.** Frameworks may be somewhat vague or very specific. Flexible or rigid. Difficult to work with or easy to adhere to. Strange or familiar. For example, an established bedtime routine can help you settle into sleep mode. A set morning routine and a healthy breakfast can help you get to school on time, ready to learn. However, everyone's bedtime and morning routines are different.

○ **Consider your comfort.** If there aren't enough guidelines for you to feel comfortable about doing a particular task, you may want to create a structure that you can work with; something that will enable you to plan, and to see progress and outcomes. There are different frameworks, so consider what will help you to be most content *and* effective in order to get the job done.[45]

○ **Be creative.** Instead of procrastinating when there's little or no structure, use your imagination to get yourself going. For example, think about a blank page. You can doodle freely, or you can draw precise geometric figures. You can fold it carefully like origami, or scrunch it, cut it, or paste stuff on it. You may be somewhat limited by the confines of the page, but you don't have to procrastinate or avoid using it. What you do within any confines is up to you. My friend Rina, an artist, says, *"Whether beginning a new painting, or starting to write a story, or sewing a quilt, the task can seem daunting and overwhelming. The only way to deal with this is* with that first step...the first stroke of a brush, the first word typed, or the first stitch...The rest will follow."[46]

○ **Be determined.** Learning to function well when there's little or no structure can be awkward or complicated. Without guidelines, you may experience trial and error, including steps in the wrong direction, or backward slip-slides. Be persistent, and push through, choosing productivity over procrastination, even when the road is uncharted or you're not sure where it's going.

○ **Sloppy success is a reality.** Curtis, a colleague, is involved in helping businesses grow, and he introduced me to the term *sloppy success*. In the business world, the best plans don't always come true, and so he says it's better to be open to the idea that unusual things sometimes happen—even when there is structure. Meetings get postponed—possibly allowing for more preparation time. In the everyday world, learning to operate without relying on perfect planning or structure can be good, too. Traffic lights malfunction—and people drive extremely cautiously. Become more accepting of the unexpected, and you'll be better prepared to know how to respond the next time things don't go your way. However, if you procrastinate, you might miss out on a sloppily successful outcome. Some of the best paintings begin with a "mess" of paint blotches. Some of the juiciest stories develop without a pre-determined framework. What can *you* create? (If you start out "sloppy," you can tidy up later.)

○ **Design a visual.** It can be helpful to see a graphic or rough diagram of the task you have to do. Try displaying the steps—beginning, middle, and end—and include any interesting ideas, and whatever materials or resources you might need. Being a self-starter means not only starting, but also continuing. A visual representation can be a good guideline, a way to keep your thoughts clear and flowing, and it works as a motivational strategy, too. Like a road map, it lets you know where you're headed.

○ **Be carefree.** If there's no structure to a task, you can always try winging it. Improvise. Get in touch with your inner self and go wherever it takes you. Rely on your instincts. Welcome the chance to dabble, experiment, and act freely.

• •

The structure you create may be uniquely yours—and that's okay. If you have a set timeline, work out how to structure it to make it feasible for you. Just plan ahead. Abraham Lincoln said, *"Give me six hours to chop down a tree, and I will spend the first four sharpening the axe."* The important thing with any timeline is first to plan so you can get the job done.

Try not to let the lack of a framework or structure cause you to procrastinate or keep you from reaching the goal of completing a task. Overcoming procrastination is a matter of *volition*—of having the will to act, instead of putting things off or avoiding them. With structure, it can be easier to move ahead because guidelines and definition help to make a process clear. However, without structure there's room for lots of creativity and outside-the-box thinking. Take hold of the possibility to devise a workable structure for yourself, letting your imagination, past experience, and know-how guide you. Go for it!

BUT...Other people keep pestering me

○ *"Do your schoolwork." "Pick up your clothes." "Put away your things." "Clean the birdcage."*

○ *"What's taking you so long?" "Why don't you ever finish what you start?" "When are you going to start that project?" "Why aren't you practicing? "What are you waiting for?"*

These are nagging demands, and questions—the finger-pointing kind that no one likes to hear.

○ *"How can I help you get started?" "What do you need to do the work?" "Should we make a plan together?" "Can I suggest a way to do that?"*

These are much better questions because they're action-based and well-intentioned. However, they can also be annoying, especially if you don't want anyone to bother you, and you'd rather be left alone.

Parents and others who see you procrastinating may mean well, but they may not know what to say, or when to say it. They want to help, but aren't sure how. Sometimes they forget to use the words, "*please*" and "*thanks*." Comments and suggestions may sound to you like commands, even though that may not be what the person intended.

Teens who talk back, act disrespectfully, or argue don't make the situation any better. When power struggles erupt, no one wins.[47]

What can you do when the adults in your life are pestering you? There are many possibilities for notching down the nagging, and also for overcoming the procrastination that lies at the core of those demanding and often accusatory comments.

• •

TIPS for when you procrastinate because others pester you

○ **Shake it off.** Like singer/composer Taylor Swift says, "*I never miss a beat, I'm lightning on my feet. And that's what they don't see, that's what they don't see.*" If you believe in yourself, even if you're not "lightning," you can still start a spark. If disbelievers or interferers are getting to you, shake it off. Take a few deep breaths. Close your eyes for minute. Hum a tune in your head to settle down. Be polite to others, but give yourself some space—to shake it off.

○ **Listen.** Pay attention to what's being said. Show that you've heard it, and say "*thank you.*" Then go on your way. However, consider thinking about the suggestions or comments. Perhaps you will learn something.

○ **Acquiesce.** That means give in. Maybe just a little. If you comply with one or two aspects of a task, and show that you're willing to make an effort, then you'll likely find the nagging will subside.

○ **Make a deal.** Talk calmly with your parents (or whoever is nagging you) about the fact that their badgering is irritating. Agree to take the first step toward doing whatever it is you're supposed to be doing if the person will agree to tone it down. Then, be honorable and follow through by taking that step toward overcoming the procrastination.

○ **De-escalate it.** Nagging involves repeatedly asking someone to do something, by way of comments, yelling, advice, or other forms of communication that are usually unpleasant. If you are on the receiving end, you could respectfully ask the person to please change their way of communicating. For example, instead of yelling, suggest that he or she leave you a note, or send you a tweet—assuming you will do your part by reading it, considering the message, and responding. Voila! Less tension.

• •

The mature thing to do when you're confronted with nagging is to think about whether there is any truth to what's being said, and to not take offense. Carefully think about your responses to other people's behavior and words before you react to them. Be tolerant. Consider the best possible way to view their comments and actions because they're probably meant to help you, even if they seem repetitive or harsh. Be aware of how your reactions might affect others, or potentially escalate a situation into an argument. Try your best to stay calm and collected. Don't be that person who heightens the uneasiness.

If parents or teachers would like to know how to help you with procrastination tendencies without pestering, you might suggest that they read *Not Now, Maybe Later.* That book gives hundreds of tips that adults can use to encourage your productivity—and perhaps even their own—in ways that don't involve pestering.

BUT...I don't have what I need (materials or support)

If you want to achieve your goals, and do so in a timely manner, then you have to have certain things handy. This might consist of desk supplies (for homework), or athletic equipment (for sports practice), or cleaning supplies (for tidying up your room). Running around searching for things can be very time consuming. Achievers and go-getters will tell you that a good tactic is to make a habit of putting together what you need ahead of time, and to have it all within easy reach. Do not squander valuable time or effort repeatedly trying to locate items (like glasses, books, keys, hats, sunscreen, tech devices, helmets, backpacks) or you will have less time to spend on meaningful pursuits.

If you procrastinate because you can't get your hands on the materials you require, that's a pretty easy fix. It's first a matter of determining where and how to get those materials. If you need help, ask for it. Be specific. You can use a checklist if you like. Pull together the items you've gathered, and position them where they're accessible. Store them carefully so you'll know exactly how to find them next time. Now you're ready to begin!

If it's support you lack, there are ways to acquire that, too. Some people procrastinate because they don't feel they can handle the workload, or cope with the expectations. (This could be their own expectations, or the expectations of others.) Others procrastinate because they want extra information or encouragement. Possibly they need guidance with one or more parts of a task—maybe at the outset or in the midst of it. In other words, they cannot do it alone, and seek the support of others. Parents, teachers, friends, and coaches—it depends on the situation. Bill Gates said, "*We all need people who will give us feedback. That's how we improve.*" Find the people who can provide that, and who can encourage you to do your best. Ask for their assistance.

Remember, "need" is a relative term. We need food, water, air, light, sleep, clothing, and safety. Those are basic fundamental needs; they help us exist, and without them our lives are endangered. Other needs include help when things seem difficult, such as reading materials, accessories and gear, and so on…Those are enabling needs that help us learn and thrive, and without them we are vulnerable. We can still function, but to a lesser degree.

Determine what needs matter most to you. They are your priorities. Put the others in perspective, and see what you can accomplish with what you have, or what you can acquire. If you have to procrastinate because of need, then your procrastination may very well be warranted. You decide.

Here are some ideas for times when you're lacking what you need in order to pursue a task.

. . . .
Tips for when you procrastinate because you lack what you need

○ **Make a color-coded list.** Categorize what you require. For example, desk supplies, resources (including people, and reading or other materials), and equipment. It's useful to have an organized system to clearly indicate what you need, and when.

○ **Ask for help in a direct way.** It's actually a sign of strength because you're showing that you're keen to learn more. Give some thought to what you want to ask. It might be a *"How to…?"* question, or a *"What is this…?"* question, or a *"Why is that…?"* question. Targeted inquiry sets the stage for specific and informative answers. Heads up: *"yes/no"* questions can yield terse *"yes/no"* answers—and those are not very informative. For example, *"Should I buy an agenda?"* is not as targeted as *"What is the best kind of agenda?"*

○ **Is it an excuse?** Do you really need stuff, or are you just using that as a way of getting out of doing something? If you need something, make an effort to get it. If you don't need it, then who are you fooling?

○ **It's not all about you.** There are others who can share their things and their ideas if only you make a polite request. This might include borrowing or exchanging books, desk materials, study notes, or whatever you need. It's helpful to offer to share your things and your ideas in return.

○ **Visualize.** Look past the "not having what I need to begin" moment, and picture the satisfaction that lies beyond. Perhaps you can start the task anyhow, in spite of not having what you need, and you can "fill in the gap" after you've begun. For example, let's say you regularly brush your teeth, rinse, and then floss. But oh my, you've run out of floss! You could procrastinate, but why? You can still brush and rinse.

○ **Improvise.** Maybe you're putting off starting an assignment because you're not sure about the instructions, and you want support. Check a similar recent assignment, or one from last year, or from a friend's class, and see if that offers some useful guidelines or ideas. Rely on wits, not on waiting. Author J. K. Rowling wrote the first Harry Potter story on notepaper, day after day, while sitting in a restaurant sipping one cup of coffee for hours. She was poor, and struggling to make ends meet, but she'd always wanted to be a writer. She used her intellect, and she did not let a lack of money or supplies stop her. She found a way to succeed, which she described as, "*You control your own life. Your own will is extremely powerful.*"

○ **Check into available support services for what you require.** Guidance counselors, school and community-based help centers, and online help desks can offer assistance. Having others to talk to or guide you can be comforting and motivating.

• •

We need opportunities to learn, and to interact with others. We need time, and patience in order to succeed. We need kindness and affection in our lives. Friends. Peace of mind. Faith. Self-respect. Purpose. And we have other needs, too. Sometimes we need medicine, forgiveness, a second chance, or a little bit of luck.[48] Everyone's needs are different. In the words of Charles Shultz (who wrote the

Peanuts comic strip), *"All you need is love. But a little chocolate now and then doesn't hurt."* And, if you're a procrastinator, perhaps what you need most is the will to succeed.

BUT...It's not fair!

What if the thing you have to do seems too difficult? Or it's due too soon? Or it has to be practically perfect? High expectations can be motivating—but they can also be troubling. Expectations can be set at school, at home, or elsewhere; by parents, teachers, friends, and coaches. Some expectations are big, or complicated, or confusing. Some seem fair and may even be flexible, whereas others seem unfair or unrealistic.

What do fair expectations look like? They're manageable, and individually targeted to suit your ability level. Not too hard, not too easy. Expectations should be right for you, and that means that they're doable in the time frame that's been set.

Fair expectations offer a chance to feel satisfaction and a sense of accomplishment once those expectations have been met. Author and professor Scott Barry Kaufman knows a lot about having a positive outlook, and he wrote these words: *"When I am around someone who I feel thinks very little of me, I tend to act little, confirming their expectations. But when I am around someone who clearly expects something good to come out of me, goodness outpours from the depths of my soul, excitedly and enthusiastically."*[49]

It's motivating when others expect good things from you, However, what's really important are the expectations that you have for yourself, based on what comes from within, and what you think is reasonable.

Fair expectations should be clear. When they're muddled, it leads to mix-ups, frustration, and time-consuming errors. Think about the expectations, and see if you can break them down and simplify them so that you can know for sure if they're fair.

Sometimes, however, we build something up in our minds, making it seem much bigger or even unattainable. Don't fret. There are ways to obtain a better perspective when you experience that kind of overblown or irrational thinking. Here are five steps that use an *ABCDE* model:[50] **1)** Start by identifying the problem or task that you have to **act** upon. What exactly is it that you're expected to do? **2)** Pay attention to the accuracy of your **beliefs** about the expectation. Is the task fair? Unfair? Why? **3)** Think about the **consequences** of your intended actions (or inaction), and the consequences of sticking to those beliefs. Could you possibly be more flexible? **4)** Get rid of irrational thinking or **dispute** it by replacing negativity and worries with a fresh outlook.[51] Perhaps there's another way to go about tackling things. **5)** Reconsider and plan an approach. The **effect** of this is that you may see the set of circumstances, problem, or task quite differently as you move forward. If it seems more doable, you'll be less likely to procrastinate! (If you revisit the bolded letters in this paragraph you'll see **A B C D E** for **A**ctions, **B**eliefs, **C**onsequences, **D**ispute, and **E**ffect. It's a mnemonic or memory device, to help you to remember this five-point strategy for coping with irrational thinking.)

When expectations are not fair, you may be tempted to lash out by arguing, procrastinating, or avoiding the task altogether. Unfair may actually mean *scary* (bungee-jumping), *difficult* (advanced math equations), *disgusting* (scrubbing toilets), *lengthy* (cleaning the cluttered garage), *ridiculous* (decorating an alphabet poster with toothpicks), *sad* (watching a movie about a sick pet), or *exhausting* (hiking along a very steep trail). These are just examples, but I mention them because I've actually experienced each of them, and even procrastinated.

In some instances, I was able to negotiate and alter the expectations. In other cases, I simply willed myself to do it, or I recruited someone else to help me or to take over some of the so-called "unfair" aspects of the job. And for tasks that were too scary (like bungee-jumping) or too exhausting (navigating precipitous pathways), I took a pass and faced the consequences. (Alas, no tale of courage while plummeting. No photos from the top of a rocky trail.)

Over time, I've learned that life is full of expectations. Sometimes we may think they're not fair, but we might be wrong about that. It helps to try and give things a chance. Maybe you can summon up the nerve or the desire or a strategy—or the benefit of the doubt—and see if you can manage it. If not, or if you're one and only go-to move is procrastination, here are some other ideas.

• •

Tips for when you procrastinate because the task is not fair

○ **Fair is not necessarily a carnival.** Not everything is jolly. Make up your mind that expectations can be fair, even though not enjoyable or fun-filled. You may have to extend yourself, or do something disagreeable or that takes a lot of time or effort. However, you can give yourself a pep talk, and plan to do something you'll enjoy after you complete the unpleasant task.

○ **Do rules have to be strictly followed?** Is it fair to have to wear a big heavy cast when you have just a tiny fracture? Is it fair to have to wait in long lines at the airport for security clearance? These are very important safety rules, and the expectations that go along with them have no flexibility. Procrastinating will not change the requirements. Other rules are not as serious, and so you may have some wiggle room. Is it fair to have to turn off your video games every evening after supper? That may be a rule that you can negotiate. Talk it over with your parents (or other rule-setter), and find out the reason for the rule, and how to make it as fair as possible for everyone. The musician Prince said, "*A strong spirit transcends rules.*" Perhaps, though it depends on the circumstances.

○ **How much time will you devote?** Let's say you've been asked to read a lengthy book, and then report on it in a single paragraph. You might think, "*It will take me several hours to do all that reading, and for what? A few short sentences!*" Realistically, it's your call as to how much time and effort you want to devote to the reading, whether you can skim through the chapters, and how much learning you want to gain from the experience. Weigh your options. What you deem to be fair may hinge on what you're willing to do, and how much time you want to spend. However, procrastinating will just add more time to the total. So, are you being fair to yourself?

○ **Are you physically able?** There's a difference between *can't* and *won't*. If you physically cannot accomplish something, then it may not be fair for others to ask you to do it. (Like climbing several flights of stairs when you have an injured knee.) However, if you *can*—but *won't*—do it, then saying, "*I can't because it's not fair!*" may not be truthful. To anyone.

○ **Start small.** Maybe the whole task seems unfair to you, but pieces of it are actually fine. Rather than procrastinating, you could begin with those. It's an opportunity for you to get ahead.

○ **It's all about the attitude.** Worms are not endangering. They're just something that I find squirmy, slimy, and gross. It's the way I think. It's my attitude. It's not "fair" for people who know this to expect me to pick up a worm and bait a hook. However, if I would be willing to take steps to change my attitude about this, then I could do it. Ultimately, it's my choice. You also can make a choice to alter your point of view about things—if you want to, and if you think it will help you to move forward and be productive.

○ **Co-create the expectations.** When you want a say in making sure that something is fair, then get involved in setting the expectations. That way you can help to ensure that they're manageable, there are reasonable timelines, the job is not offensive, and that it's worth doing.

• •

Fair is a relative term. What's fair to one person may not be fair to another. If you have to justify why something is not fair, keep that in mind. Not everyone is liable to agree with you.

Moreover, if you opt to procrastinate because something is unfair, then there may be consequences. Be prepared, because you may not think those are fair either...

BUT...What about my friends?

Friends can bring out the best in you. Good friends let you be yourself. They're patient. They defend you. They offer comfort. They're understanding.

We trust that our friends will be there in times of difficulty, when we have stuff to get done, when we need someone to confide in, or when we're not sure what direction to take. Friends help us as we travel through life. Philosopher Albert Camus beautifully captured that idea by saying, *"Don't walk behind me; I may not lead. Don't walk in front of me; I may not follow. Just walk beside me and be my friend."* Side-by-side. That's what friendship is all about.

However, sometimes friends ask us to do things—or not do things. Or they're hard to keep up with. Other times, friends leave us wondering what to do, and sometimes what they want us to do is unwise. Peer pressure is something that lots of teens deal with on a daily basis, and they may be tempted to "follow" various behaviors or choices. These might have to do with music, clothes, extracurricular activities, social networks, or how to approach home and school responsibilities.

You may not want to let on if you can't do something, or if you feel it's too simple, or if it's not cool. You may be embarrassed about not wanting to go along with others. However, you shouldn't have to do anything that you think is unsafe or improper, or makes you uncomfortable. It's okay to back off.

Remember, you don't have to compare what you do or accomplish to what your friends do or accomplish. It's important to do what you instinctively like and feel good about. That will lead to progress and ultimately accomplishment on your part, regardless of what your friends might be up to.

Friends can also be positive influences. They can help you if you're having trouble getting things done, or if you're uncertain how to begin a task. Here are some more considerations having to do with friends.

. . . .
Tips for when you procrastinate
because of issues with friends

○ **Do you get caught up in someone else's net?** Be true to yourself. If your friends put things off, you don't have to do that. If they expect you to do things you disapprove of or aren't happy about, you don't have to do that either. If your friends are having difficulties, you can listen, and often even offer to help. That's what friends do.

○ **Friends are resources.** Look to your friends to give you emotional support and encouragement when you need it. Sometimes, we need others to reassure us that we're capable, and that what we do is worth doing. Poet E. E. Cummings said these memorable words, *"We do not believe in ourselves until someone reveals that deep inside us something is valuable, worth listening to, worthy of our trust, sacred to our touch. Once we believe in ourselves, we can risk curiosity, wonder, spontaneous delight or any experience that reveals the human spirit."* Let your friends help you to believe more strongly in yourself, and you, in turn, can encourage them.

○ **Are you a procrastination piggy-backer?** Friends who procrastinate may have good reason—but these reasons are theirs, not yours. Regardless of what's causing them to put things off, it may actually have nothing to do with you. If you're going to procrastinate, then make sure the reason is relevant to you, and that you're not just copying someone else's behavior.

○ **So, you like geocaching...**(High-tech reality scavenger hunts.) Or maybe you enjoy escape rooms, playing chess, cosplay, or drawing in an intricate coloring book. But what if your friends don't like to do any of these things? Do you follow your interests, or not? Rather than procrastinating or shying away from doing the things you enjoy, you could give your friends a little information, or alternatively, suggest they investigate the options for themselves. However, don't let their lack of interest dissuade you from pursuing yours. Live your dreams.

○ **Friends can keep you really busy.** Too busy? It's wonderful to hang out with friends. Sometimes time passes quickly, and before you know it there's none left for the homework, chores, or other activities that you were planning to do. You might be tempted to blame others, but it's not really their fault. When you know you have responsibilities, you need to create a strategy. Set aside a certain amount of time to be with your friends, and plan to stop at a specific point so that you can meet other commitments. Ask your friends to help you if you don't think you can stick to your plan.

○ **Jokes can sting.** Sometimes friends make jokes with one another about their shortcomings or tendencies. If people poke fun at you because you always hand things in past the due date, or you're late getting places, or you can't be counted on to do your part of a group project, there may be a lot of truth in their so-called jokes. If their words sting, chances are the joke is not really funny. And if no one is laughing, or they're laughing *at* you rather than *with* you, then pay attention and show them you're willing to try to change. However, if a joking situation deteriorates into bullying, that becomes a more serious matter. Those who get caught up—whether as victim or bully—may need help learning not to take offense or not to go on the offense too quickly. Either way, there are resources and support systems you can tap if bullying experiences are a problem for you.[52]

○ **What's your group dynamic?** We typically make friends with people who share our interests, and with whom we can relate and relax. Togetherness can be a benefit but also a liability. Do you hang out with perfectionists? Worriers? Procrastinators? Gamers? There's an old saying, "*Birds of a feather flock together.*" What kind of "flock" are you a part of? Do your friends inspire you (and you them), or do you waste time or keep one another from soaring? Who takes the lead? Can you?

○ **New friends bring new possibilities.** You may have dear friends who will be part of your life forever. I have many friends from my long-ago nursery and elementary school days, and I value and enjoy these friendships. But…they are not my only friends. It's good to branch out, and to continue to make new friends. It does not mean you're devaluing the "old" ones. By taking advantage of opportunities to connect with additional people you'll build a broader support system, learn different ways to do things, and increase your collaborative options. Relationships foster fresh perspectives, and renewed strength.

○ **Enlist a support team.** Perhaps you find it difficult to begin tasks, but you're generally good to go once you actually get going. Or maybe you're okay at starting things, and then lose momentum. What's your pattern? Once you figure that out, or if you can predict that a certain task is going to pose problems at a particular point, you could ask your friends to give you extra encouragement when you really need it.

• •

Your friends are important, and if you're lucky, you will cherish one another for many, many years. It's great to be able to spend time together. However, if this leaves you little or no time to do other things, and if you're missing out on opportunities, or if you're falling behind at school, then you might want to think carefully about how your friends can pitch in and help you become more productive.

BUT…There are too many technological demands

Technology has infused all aspects of life. We carry devices everywhere, relying on them for communication, direction, entertainment, and information. Web-based activities, social media, Instagram, texts—they're time-consuming. They can be distracting, too.

Technology has many pluses. For example, video games can help people learn explicit skills such as problem-solving and decision-making. Apps provide shortcuts and resources that are designed to make our lives easier. Tech voices speak to us, wake us up, answer questions, and provide explanations. We listen, watch, and learn. However, too much of anything may not be wise or healthy.

On the other hand, too little technology can also be problematic. Toddlers tap their way to knowledge, teachers depend on computer-based activities, and teens are expected to be savvy. Those who aren't up to what is expected may find themselves at a disadvantage. Too little tech-use can be as detrimental as too much.

And, about games...So many, all kinds, and very tempting. Gaming, and connecting with other gamers, can take up a lot of precious time. Games are entertaining and command attention, and before you know it the morning, afternoon, or evening has flown by.

In order to manage the amount of cutting-edge technology you use from day to day, it's useful to figure out when you find it valuable, and when you'd be better off withdrawing from it. For example, two hours spent on Facebook or on the Internet may not be time well spent, whereas two hours familiarizing yourself with an e-book on time management may, indeed, be helpful and worthwhile for you.

There has been much written about how much time spent online is "suitable" for kids of different ages, and how to handle overload concerns.[53] And, there have been studies about the importance of reducing teens' screen time so they can become more focused on what matters elsewhere.[54] Here are some suggestions to help you get unplugged, whether it's a little or a lot.

• •

Tips for when you procrastinate because of technological demands

○ **Entertainment or learning applications?** What's your pleasure? How do you use your devices? There are countless online programs, resources, and educational tools—for example, peer editing, connectivity with experts in various fields, and ways to pool ideas. But there's also the allure of YouTube and social media channels, and the incessant barrage of information of all kinds. When using devices, think about the *purpose*, and try to separate "academic" intent (such as using learning tools) from "non-educational" intent (such as using entertainment-based activities). Focus on one application, then the other, not both at once.

○ **Multi-tasking is an acquired skill.** Smart phones, television screens, and gaming consoles can pull you away from your responsibilities. Kids learn to multi-task at a young age, but when people do two, three, or sometimes four things at once, some tasks suffer as a result. Ask other people what tricks they use in order to multitask more efficiently and get things done. For example, you might keep a pad of paper handy to jot things down for later, and you could clear stuff off your desktop so you have less visible clutter to deal with.

○ **Technology makes things too easy.** Sometimes a task is so simple that it doesn't seem worth doing. If it's only going to take a short time, and there's a familiar app for it or a technological short cut, then there's probably no rush to get started. However, if you decide to procrastinate, be sure to leave enough time in case the task turns out to be more complicated than you thought.

○ **Use the calendar or schedule on your device.** When making entries, it's helpful to think about budgeting your time, giving yourself as much as you need for each task or activity. Be sure to consider when things are due, and think carefully about how much potential extra time you just might need for each step along the way as you make entries in your calendar. Beware the "maybe" option offered within most of these apps. If something is unconfirmed or uncertain, you don't have to fall prey to it. And, consider working backward from the due date if that's easier for you.

○ **Be specific as to what's due, and when.** Seeing "assignment due" pop up again and again on your screen is like being trapped in a relentless and overwhelming cycle of procrastination. The message may be intended to remind you, but it's vague, repetitive, and annoying. Is the assignment a book review? A math test? A lab report? A creative writing project? Mark down exactly what it is, and when it is due. That way you'll know for sure and you'll be less inclined to tune out the reminder.

○ **Try Things.** (Or try other similar things…) Things is a task manager program that's easy to use. You can enter everything you have to do and get organized so you can tackle one goal at a time.

○ **Turn it off!** Headphones, smartphones, electronic tablets—personal Internet-enabled devices are everywhere. It may be hard, but you can periodically distance yourself from them, and also from the Internet. There's a program called Freedom that allows you to block access. There's also something called an OFF switch.

○ **Enkrateia vs akrasia?** The ancient past and the digital age converge! With a couple of taps on my computer I learned that Greek philosophers had interesting views about having power over oneself (*enkrateia*), versus lacking self-control and going against one's better judgment (*akrasia*). I ended up reading about resolutions, weakness of will, different kinds of motivation, and conflicts between reason and emotion. One link led to another. Endlessly. Leaving me with a choice to carry on investigating (and thus put off other things), or to skim and move on. This is just one example of how the Internet can lead us on a never-ending chase of information—if we let it. Once you have enough information for now (say one or two pages of relevant facts), resolve to put it aside. Or, alternatively, set yourself a time limit and stick to it. Harness your *enkrateia*!

• •

Electronic devices provide wonderful resources, and creative and interactive learning experiences. However, it's up to the people who use them to think, and to put their time to good use. At the end of the day—any day—the choice is yours whether to be tech-no-smart or distracted. You are a consumer of information with tons of opportunities at your fingertips. What you tap into, and when you tap into it, will inevitably affect how your day unfolds, and what you will or won't accomplish. Keep in mind that even the tiniest taps can lead in many different, time-consuming, or unexpected directions. Remember, too, that no matter how sophisticated technology gets, there are still only 24 hours in a day. Use your time wisely. Getting ahead is not just about technology. In the words of author Mark Twain, *"The secret of getting ahead is getting started."* (Granted, he didn't have a computer or handheld electronic device back in his day—1835-1910—but the advice is still rock solid!)

BUT...My parents procrastinate

Very likely, your family is like your own personal cheerleading squad or home team. That doesn't mean they should be doing everything for you, but it does mean they probably have your back when you get into difficult situations. However, it's unfair to take advantage of them by acting helpless, or lazy, or disrespectful of their good graces. They'll lose patience with you if you complain or cajole or expect them to bail you out a LOT—especially when you're capable of doing things for yourself. With that said, if you are truly in need of help, and if you find yourself stuck, family members can be wonderfully supportive. They know you well, and when you're going nowhere, they can help push you forward with just the right kind of assistance and encouragement.

Of course, not all family members are immediately responsive. They may take a while to make their move. Lots of teens have parents (or grandparents, or older siblings) who procrastinate at various times, yet manage just fine overall. If they can put things off, or even avoid them, and still do okay, why can't you? How bad can procrastination be?

Hmmm. You might want to ask your family members, *"What do you think you might have missed out on because you procrastinate?"* Find out what kinds of opportunities may have passed them by. Money? Jobs? The joy of achievements never realized? Has their procrastination led to anxious feelings, or strained relationships with other people? Your parents may be doing okay, but what if they didn't procrastinate? Would they be doing better? Their comments could inspire you to be more productive than they are, or have been.

Family support can be especially helpful when you feel your life is a chaotic muddle, consisting of incomplete or late assignments and far too much to do. You know those times, when your stomach is in knots or your head aches, and there's the pending doom of forgotten books, misplaced papers, looming deadlines, and other stuff hanging over you like a dark cloud. But, your parents and others within your family circle have probably had days or weeks like that, too. Their advice can help you to become more organized and less frantic.

Parents and others who procrastinate may do so all the time (chronically), or every once in a while (periodically). So, what you *see* when other people procrastinate may not really reflect what's going on in their minds or their lives. You don't know the whole story. And, likewise, what they see when you procrastinate might not be a true picture of what you're thinking or what's happening in your life. It's helpful to talk with one another about procrastination, including the reasons for it, and whether they're good reasons (justified) or bad (cop-outs). Chat about how you can support each other when tempted to procrastinate. Share ideas for improving organization and time management, and for overcoming challenges. Your family can be a huge source of strength, and help keep you on track.

• •

Tips for when you procrastinate because your parents do

○ **What strategies work well within your family?** Do your parents have any suggestions to help you overcome procrastination? Do they have any tips to provide you with a more structured outlook? Are sticky notes plastered across the refrigerator a useful strategy? Does teaming up help? For example, if your mother is an author (like me), she may have a writing partner—someone she can rely on, and who will encourage her efforts. Writing partners can share the load when it's time to compose a lengthy article, create an index, or write about a topic that is not particularly appealing. Having a coauthor on some projects keeps me productive and accountable. I respect my partner; she's a friend and a colleague, and I would never let her down. Therefore, when I write (even when I do so independently), I've learned not to procrastinate! What can your parents teach you from their work-based experiences? How do they handle tasks?

○ **Respect your own internal clock.** Take a moment or two for a reality check and to listen to your inner voice. You know when you work best, and feel most energized, so you may be most comfortable sticking to that timeframe. However, your alert time of day may not be the same as that of your parents. For instance, your father may have a tendency to procrastinate in the morning, whereas you may have a hard time getting things done in the evenings. Be respectful of other people's preferences, routines, and differences, and talk about those, and about yours. A discussion may reveal ways to maximize productivity at various times throughout the day.

○ **Parents get maxed out, too, you know.** At work, at home, and coming and going—parents are busy juggling overlapping or double-booked activities, pick-ups, drop-offs, overflowing inboxes, grocery shopping, and many other responsibilities. It may look like your parents are procrastinating when they won't help you with something right away. Keep in mind your parents may be doing as much as they can while trying to deal with jam-packed and potentially stressful schedules. Cut them some slack, and be careful not to be too quick to judge them as procrastinators, or to point to their procrastination as a reason for *you* to put things off.

○ **Problem-solve together.** There may be things that you, your parents, or siblings could do around the house to make it easier for everyone to be more efficient. For example, upgrading the family's computer software, posting a color-coded family calendar, creating a monthly household to-do list, or recycling stuff that causes clutter and disorganization. These solutions could help make things run smoothly, prevent misunderstandings about who should do what and when, and create a more cohesive family lifestyle.

○ **Roll with crisis-driven decisions.** Sometimes your parents have to deal suddenly or unexpectedly with something really important, and as a result other (also) important things get left undone. For instance, an illness, a critical message, or a power failure could force them to change their plans. This is not procrastination; it's coping. If your parents are putting things off due to unexpected occurrences, try to be patient. You may even be able to help. And remember, everything is not about you.

○ **Modify the home environment by reducing distractions.** Work together with your family to minimize recurring distractions around the house. A group effort can be motivating. You know how you're tempted to eat cookies or chips when they're left out on the counter? People are more likely to be taken off course or to procrastinate when there are snacks, games, and other visible diversions close by. Relocate them. Cooperate with one another and devise an action plan. Altering the environment for even a short time each day may help everyone become more productive.

○ **Have regular family meetings.** Regularly might mean once or twice a week, maybe more or less. Work it out and then be consistent. Talk about what's on the calendar. What needs to be done? By whom? By when? What has to be added or crossed off? How can you help or encourage one another to get started? What distractions should you eliminate? Alongside time for work, is there also time for relaxation and family fun?

• •

Your parents and other family members have many good qualities. So instead of thinking about their procrastination tendencies, think about their other wonderful traits. Like honesty, kindness, creativity…What do you admire most in your parents? What can you emulate? Appreciate their virtues. Be open to learning from all their characteristics, behavior, wise words, and experiences. Be open to the power of possibility—which just so happens to be the starting point for the final chapter of this book.

CHAPTER 5

But What If...?

"Optimism is the faith that leads to achievement.
Nothing can be done without hope and confidence."
~ Helen Keller (author and humanitarian
who was both deaf and blind)

The power of possibility

If you want to prevent, manage, or eliminate your procrastination, the hundreds of tips throughout this book will give you starting points. Ironically, however, the problem with that is if you tend to procrastinate (which is what this book is all about), then how do you start? It's kind of a vicious circle, like that age-old question about what came first, the chicken or the egg?

Don't despair, because there is always the power of possibility! You can go back through the pages of this book and review your key points by thinking about the particular BUTS...that concern you. For example, are you overwhelmed? Bored? Confused? Disorganized? Distracted? Consider the strategies that might work for you, personally, based on a desire to improve your productivity—whether it's by overcoming a possible weakness or by bolstering possible strengths.

If you don't want to do that, or none of the strategies helps, then it's possible the issue you have to confront is not just procrastination. Yes, you may lack the inclination or drive to start things,

123

but you may also be lacking motivation on a larger scale. There is motivation to *learn*, and motivation to *achieve*. Do you want to learn? Do you want to achieve? Ask yourself, because the answer to this could be at the heart of what's causing you to put things off. If your answer is "*no*," and you really have no interest in propelling yourself forward, you might require more focused and professional attention than you can acquire by just reading through a how-to book like this. Talk with your parents or a trusted adult about your lack of motivation and possible next steps. If you think you need more help, then don't hesitate to ask for it.

Overcoming procrastination is really a goal. Think of it as a particular objective or target. If you're willing to put forth some effort (with an emphasis on both will and effort), then you're ready to try and hit that target. And as with motivation, there are *learning* goals and *achievement* goals.

Learning goals have to do with gaining new skills and under-standings, including looking for and finding strategies to increase your abilities. Achievement goals have to do with performance and outcomes, including gaining positive judgments about your abilities. Both types of goals fuel motivation because, in reality, everyone, regardless of age, wants to be validated for skills, knowledge, and accomplishments. But focusing on the goal is not the only consideration. It's also important to pay attention to the process—the "getting there" part. It can motivate you, and be pleasurable, too.

Procrastination interferes with motivation. It can also interfere with happiness, success, relationships, and overall well-being. It's important to find ways to reduce its hold and impact on your life. I hope you will continue to do that.

The heading of this section is "the power of possibility," but what is that power? It's not about wishing on a star, or making dreams come true, or the vague or even hokey kinds of things people sometimes say, like "*Work hard, play hard!*" The power of possibility lies in the practical application. I think Saint Francis of Assisi captured the essence of possibility in these words, "*Start by doing what's necessary; then do what's possible; and suddenly you are doing the impossible.*" A similar quote is from Nobel Prize winner and statesman Nelson Mandela, who said, "*It always seems impossible until it's done.*" For people who find procrastination challenging—who find it impossible to get started, or difficult to advance or stay on task—the advice about beginning by doing what is "necessary" (essential, urgent, required) makes excellent sense.

So, what is necessary? For me, it's family ties. Safety. Physical and mental health. Personal integrity. Happiness. Friendships. That's just a short list. What's necessary for *you* to look after first and foremost?

People can create their own lists, and they will differ in content and length. Knowing what you have to pay attention to now, rather than later, is a very solid first step. It can lead to other steps and possibilities. Think about what things you need to make that first step happen, and who can help you do that. Where and when you go after that is ultimately up to you. Once you rise to the occasion, start to move forward, and get past procrastinating, you'll be primed to keep going. And that's the power of possibility!

What if all else fails? (20 Don'ts)

Throughout this book I've offered practical suggestions—points that emphasize things you can DO to overcome procrastination. DOING is hugely important. British Prime Minister Margaret Thatcher said, "*Disciplining yourself to do what you know is right and important, although difficult, is the highroad to pride, self-esteem, and personal satisfaction.*"

Here I focus on DON'TS—twenty brief but important suggestions consisting of pitfalls to avoid if you really want to put an end to procrastinating.

1. **Don't deceive yourself.** Figure out why you're procrastinating, what you're feeling, and what you can do—with or without help.

2. **Don't get yourself down.** Be positive, and think beyond the present moment to the satisfaction that you'll feel once you get going and accomplish something. Lighten up. Give yourself a pep talk.

3. **Don't try to do too much all at once**. Go step by step by step. And the steps don't have to be big. Focus on the journey, not on the destination.

4. **Don't give up.** Don't cave in, hold off, or let other people bail you out. When you encounter challenge or difficulty, show determination and resilience.

5. **Don't set multiple goals.** Set one manageable goal at a time, with reasonable intervals and timelines for completion.

6. **Don't neglect your health and well-being.** Look after yourself. Get enough sleep, eat properly, and make time for relaxation and play. You won't be productive if you're tired, malnourished, or wound up.

7. **Don't do it alone.** Share the load with others.

8. **Don't be hesitant about asking questions.** If you're procrastinating because you aren't sure about how to do something, ask. Parents, teachers, family members, and friends can assist you.

9. **Don't ignore your energy levels.** Pay attention to when you work most efficiently, and take advantage of those times.

10. **Don't ignore your strengths.** Tap into what you do well—for example, your interests, skills, curiosity, past successes, and creativity.

11. **Don't underestimate the value of routines.** They help you stay on course. You'll feel more comfortable, and you'll be less likely to procrastinate when things are familiar and established.

12. **Don't get sidetracked by distractions.** Video games, snacks, television programs, music, text messages, snapchat, phone calls, the Internet…? What typically interferes with your productivity? Put it away for periods of time.

13. **Don't be afraid to take a risk or to make mistakes.** You'll learn from overcoming difficulty and coping with errors and setbacks.

14. **Don't get into a confrontation with parents or teachers.** Battles don't prove anything, and they're upsetting. It makes more sense to be patient, to communicate, and to listen to one another. Step back from the front lines, and don't fight.

15. **Don't make comparisons.** If friends or family members procrastinate—or alternatively, complete things really quickly—well, that's *them* and you're *you*. Work out a plan or timeline that suits your needs and preferences, and don't be tied to other people's behavior, or to what they do or do not accomplish.

16. **Don't forget to reward yourself.** A smoothie. A sleep in. A few minutes playing a video game. Give yourself a little boost once you've gotten past procrastinating. Incentives can be motivating.

17. **Don't dismiss shortcuts.** If something seems daunting or time-consuming, consider taking a shortcut rather than procrastinating. Is there a faster or more efficient approach you can try? You don't want to compromise quality but you don't want to squander your energy or time either.

18. **Don't forget the tools.** What do you need? It might be a calendar, an agenda, an electronic planner, a well-equipped desk, a timer...Make sure you have the stuff you require to get the job(s) done.

19. **Don't devalue what matters to you.** You may have good reasons for procrastinating, or doing what you want, when you want. Commit to your choices, and see them through, although you might also want to be prepared to defend them. When you accomplish what you want, you'll respect yourself, and feel more confident.

20. **Don't lose faith in yourself.** Believe in your capabilities. You can do anything you put your mind to!

Where to look for more information

Sometimes you may need extra help or resources, and there are several links and suggestions in this final segment. I've separated it into three sections for easy reference: 1) more about motivation, 2) more about time management, and 3) more about developing personal strengths.

1) More about motivation

Top motivators for teens

When people are motivated to do something, they are less likely to procrastinate. Motivation is the key to action. If you "swing for the fence," you're liable to hit a home run. If you don't swing the bat at all, you'll strike out.

In my Educational Psychology classes at the University of Toronto, I've encouraged hundreds of prospective high school teachers to think about their own experiences as students, and to reflect upon what they read and learn about motivation and academic success. I invite each aspiring teacher to come up with a "top ten list" of surefire motivators; that is, what they think would motivate their students to get things done. Over the past decade I've collected tons of suggestions, and here are 30 of them that I like a lot, in random order. I share these motivators courtesy of all those would-be educators who have since graduated, and are now teaching in various places. (Maybe even at your school!)

○ Positive feelings such as excitement and happiness

○ Choice

○ Breaks and time out for rest or relaxation

○ Music, art, drama, and other creative, artistic approaches

○ Being able to do something the way you want

○ Change of scenery, outings, field trips, fresh air and sunshine

○ Opportunities to socialize, play, and collaborate with others

○ Knowing it's alright to make mistakes, and that help is available

○ Speakers or guests who offer new points of view

○ Novelty

○ Inspirational quotes or stories

○ Upbeat, positive, enthusiastic attitudes of others

○ Routines and familiarity

○ Manageability—not too easy and not too hard

○ Honest and constructive feedback

○ Flexibility

○ Chance to become a leader, to increase strengths

○ Relevance, usefulness, connections to daily life (such as culture and interests)

○ Interesting and fair assessment processes and marking schemes

○ Being asked—and also being encouraged to ask—intelligent questions

○ Intriguing or challenging problems to solve

○ Invitations to help create workable timelines and due dates

○ Healthy competition, such as trying to break records or surmount barriers

○ Wanting to do something well enough to be able to teach it to others

○ Rewards or incentives

○ Breaking things down into steps to tackle one at a time

○ Physical activity, being able to move around

○ Technology as part of the mix

○ Surprise, intrigue, having curiosity piqued

○ Fun

My sincere thanks to all the teachers who shared their top motivators, and whose tips appear here.

Inspirational reading

There are many wonderful books about teens who face challenges or put things off, and who become motivated in different and often unexpected ways. Biographies of people who have succeeded after overcoming difficulties can also be motivating. Perhaps a librarian, teachers, friends, or family can suggest stories (and songs, movies, plays, speeches, or poems) that feature real or fictional characters that have inspired them.

Have you ever heard of The Hero's Journey? It's a fascinating outline that depicts how stories are structured, with consistent rules that create a format that's typically about human needs and conquests. The 12-point framework explains what a story's main character experiences from the starting point of a journey, when confronting obstacles, and while being motivated to overcome challenges and continue forth until reaching the end goal. Here are the 12 points:

1) ordinary world
2) call to adventure
3) refusal of the call
4) meeting the mentor
5) crossing the threshold
6) test, allies, and enemies
7) approach the innermost cave
8) the central ordeal
9) the reward
10) the road back
11) resurrection
12) return with elixir

This format can be seen in myths, modern action tales, or even fairytales. You can go online to see a broad and colorful array of creative designs that illustrate The Hero's Journey.[55] The designs include general concept maps, and ones that show how the structure applies to specific stories such as *The Hobbit, Star Wars, Harry Potter, Indiana Jones, The Hunger Games, Hercules,* and on and on…(To provide a simple example, I've chosen a story that is familiar to all—*Cinderella*—so you can see in the endnotes how the structure plays out.[56])

So, what does The Hero's Journey have to do with motivation? The 12-point outline can help you to identify what story characters do, and what strategies they use as they strive to reach their goals. Do they procrastinate? Sometimes they do. And their reasons for putting things off may be valid, or feeble, or silly—or any one of the reasons outlined throughout the pages of *Bust Your BUTS*…But ultimately, the stories are resolved, and the hero's journey comes to an end. If you look at the various journeys, you will discover the different ways characters reached their goals, including what tools, tips, and tricks they drew upon to keep motivated, so they could prevail, even when demands or setbacks were at their most challenging.

Think of these words, *"You must do the very thing you think you cannot do."*[57]

Pick a story that you think might help you to better appreciate this quote, and to perhaps gain inspiration from the Hero's Journey. Here are several of my favorite titles. You can add yours to the list:

The Phantom Tollbooth—by Norton Juster
Charlotte's Web—by E. B. White
The Little Prince—by Antoine de Saint Exupéry
The Lion, the Witch, and the Wardrobe—by C. S. Lewis
Tuck Everlasting—by Natalie Babbitt
To Kill a Mockingbird—by Harper Lee
The Catcher in the Rye—by J. D. Salinger
The Book Thief—by Markus Zusak
The Fault in Our Stars—by John Green
All the Light We Cannot See—by Anthony Doerr
Grapes of Wrath—by John Steinbeck
The Color Purple—by Alice Walker
The Hobbit—by J. R. R. Tolkien

You will find titles such as these and more on the lists of all-time favorite books for young people—some selected by the librarians at the New York Public Library, others recommended by The College Board (which has compiled a list of "101 Great Books Recommended for College-Bound Readers").[58] TIME has also published lists of top books for kids, and a collection of suggestions for young adults, too.[59]

Brain-building experiences

Activities that inform and stimulate thinking, like reading books—and appreciating their messages—can be motivating. Challenging extracurricular activities can also have terrific motivational impact. What kinds of opportunities exist in your neighborhood?[60]

The brain-building ideas that follow next are variations of ones presented in a checklist in *Beyond Intelligence: Secrets for Raising Happily Productive Kids*. Each of these ideas presents plenty of opportunities for conversations, creative interactions, and inquiry (just ask who, what, where, why, when, and how as you go). Remember, if something connects meaningfully with your life, then you will be motivated to begin, and more likely to stay engaged. Here are a dozen activities that can promote various kinds of meaningful connections.

- Inventive activities—robotics, building structures, making costumes, designing stage sets

- Museums—history, discovery, science, athletic

- Performances—plays, sing-alongs, orchestras, concerts, improvs, karaoke

- Art experiences—sculpting, collages, drawing, gallery visits, painting, origami

- Shops—food, clothing, hardware, groceries, antiques, electronics

- Neighborhood walks—past interesting buildings, people, playgrounds

- Nature walks—parks, conservation areas, beaches, gardens, ponds, orchards

- Kitchen activities—cooking, experimenting, eating

- Photography—taking pictures, sorting, arranging, creating albums

- Sports—team, individual (participating and watching)

- Play—outdoor, structured and unstructured

- Travel—real and close, virtual and far

If you want to be motivated (as in not procrastinate), look for some excitement, relevance, value, or fun. If the task is manageable, then the onus is on you to put forth the effort required to complete it. Think about your past successes, and about the determination and motivators you tapped in order to achieve those successes. Build upon this, and try to generate some enthusiasm. Poet Ralph Waldo Emerson said, *"Nothing great was ever achieved without enthusiasm."* By harnessing enthusiasm and pushing yourself forward you can change your world, one action and one day at a time.

2) More about time management

Drawing the line

Everyone has exactly the same number of hours per day. Scientists, humanitarians, athletes, artists—no one is graced with more than 24 hours. Yet some individuals achieve so much more than others. People can organize and use time productively, or they can waste many or most of their allotted hours, 365 days a year.

Picture this: The International Date Line is a "real" but imaginary navigational line on the Earth's surface. It runs invisibly from the North Pole to the South Pole, and marks the change of one calendar day to the next. The IDL passes through the middle of the Pacific Ocean, and swerves and deviates so it doesn't go directly through any of the island nations in the vicinity.

However, what if the International Date Line ran through your kitchen? Aside from the fact that you'd be able to enjoy a double birthday celebration, you'd have a constant excuse if you didn't want to do something. You could claim, *"I'll do it tomorrow!"* knowing full well that tomorrow would depend on when (or if) you chose to cross the line.

You draw the line (albeit not the actual IDL) in your own home. You decide what you will and will not do, and how you'll manage the time you have at your disposal each day. You can procrastinate and come up with excuses galore. (*"I wasn't sure what day it was." "My homework blew away in a big gust of wind, and then a squirrel ran off with it." "The assignment fell behind the desk, and I couldn't move the furniture."*) Or, you can set about doing whatever you have to do. Remember, your integrity and your reputation will follow you as you go through life, and they are important assets. Do you really want to take a chance that will compromise them?

Organizational strategies

In order to be prepared, it helps to be organized and "planful." Albert Einstein said, *"By failing to prepare you are preparing to fail."*

Preparation and planning involve creating a well-ordered action framework. It will provide direction, and a workable time-line—and also the comforting sense that you know where you're going, how you're going to get there, and what you can do to make the process as carefree as possible. If you have a sensible and organized framework in place (and procrastination is not part of your plan!), then you will be inclined to be more industrious.

Lots of people research and write about organizational strategies. Much of the material typically includes suggestions like these:

○ Use a planner (agenda) and a master family calendar.

○ Establish consistent routines for homework, bedtime, and other tasks and activities.

○ Create a designated supply depot for easy access of the stuff you use often.

○ Buddy up so that you're accountable to someone in addition to yourself.

○ Use containers, folders, desk caddies, and closet organizers to categorize things and keep them together.

○ Create checklists and keep them up to date.

○ Prepare for the day ahead.

○ Try apps such as Wunderlist, Any.do, and Evernote.

○ Watch what your parents and other people do to get and stay organized, and learn from them.

○ Set aside a weekly check-point time to assess where you are with your various commitments, and to make sure you haven't veered off course.

Habits and practical tactics

Here's an overview of three time management books that you might find useful.

1. Consistent habits can be helpful if you're looking to manage your time and overcome procrastination tendencies. Sean Covey writes about habits that help teens become more efficient and productive.[61] In sharing some of his ideas here, I've taken the liberty of condensing material, and bolding specific words that I believe represent key concepts:

    ○ **Take responsibility** for choices and consequences, actions, and outcomes.

    ○ Have a vision, and **make an action plan** so you'll know where you're headed.

    ○ **Prioritize** based on importance; first things first.

    ○ **Collaborate** with others; share ideas and strategies, and propel one another forward.

    ○ **Be caring**—that is, be open-minded, seeking to understand as well as to be understood.

○ **Capitalize on your strengths** in order to stay on track and do your utmost.

○ Make time to relax and re-energize so you can **feel balanced**, and so you'll be able to focus on what you need to do

2. New York Times bestselling Author Kevin Kruse wrote *15 Secrets Successful People Know about Time Management*, which offers useful tips that focus on some surprising things ultra-productive people do differently.[62] Kruse bases his information on interviews with thousands of people—professionals, entrepreneurs, Olympic athletes, straight-A students, billionaires, and more. I've summarized and adapted Kruse's material here, and present a rough overview of his list of 15 things productive people do in order to be productive.

○ **Focus on minutes.** There are 1,440 minutes per day. What can you accomplish in a 60 second interval? (Eat some fruit. Call a friend and say a quick hello. Reflect upon a memory. Apologize. Wash your dishes. Stretch. Hum a happy tune. Or…) Do you use your 1,440 minutes wisely?

○ **Set daily priorities.** Identify your one most important task (MIT) and set aside time for it—for example, every morning. Stick to it.

○ **Toss your to-do list.** Use a calendar instead.

○ **Consider imaginary time travel.** Think—what can you do now to make sure that your "future self" does the right thing? How can you set things in motion in a good way?

○ **Block in your priorities.** Make time for dinner and family togetherness.

○ **Use a notebook to capture ideas.** To-do's go on the calendar.

○ **Limit e-mail activity**. Check it only three times a day. Schedule times to read and respond.

○ **Avoid meetings.** If a meeting is necessary, keep it short and encourage people to stand up.

○ **Learn to say no.** Say no to everything outside your goal areas.

○ **Follow the 80/20 rule.** 80% of outcomes come from 20% of activities. Identify the 20%, and make an effort to ignore the rest.[63]

○ **Delegate or outsource almost everything.** Identify your abilities, use them, and outsource other things.

○ **Theme each day of the week.** Create a schedule, and focus on a major area each day, making a single batch of stuff to deal with.

○ **Go for fast and immediate.** If it will only take 10 minutes to complete, do it now.

○ **Create a morning ritual.** Wake up early and take an hour or so every morning for your spiritual, mental, and physical health.

○ **Focus on energy, not time.** In order to maximize productivity, pay attention to your sleep, nutrition, exercise, and breaks during the day.

3. Mitzi Weinman also offers advice to individuals and families who want to "find time" to use productively, and with one another.[64] In her blog, and in her book *It's About Time,* Weinman provides practical strategies, and discusses the importance of developing good habits. She also offers student webinars on organization.

    Weinman suggests that family members do an inventory of time spent together, including assessing the following:

○ Importance—Does time spent doing activities align with what matters in each family member's life? Based on:
—Clarity (Are priorities clear?)
—Agreement (Do you agree with the priorities?)

○ Homework—Is there enough time, at a "good" time, when teens can focus?

○ Unstructured time—Have you scheduled time for recreation and to relax?

Time spent with family can be lots of fun, plus it can strengthen bonds, motivation, resilience, and resolve.

3) More about developing personal strengths

Cool heads prevail

If you make up your mind to get things done, and if you take a deep breath and exude purpose and self-confidence, there is no end to what you can accomplish. Opportunity knocks in different ways (including softly, harshly, and unexpectedly), but you have to be willing to answer that knock.

Very early in this book, I discuss the importance of being calm. This is really important because it enables you to be in the right frame of mind to both hear and respond to any knock. Pause and collect your thoughts. If demands are worrisome, or things are piling up, and you're tempted to procrastinate, it helps to reflect and take stock of what's what around you. This includes people's feelings, and the potential consequences of any actions you might take. Try deep breathing, exercising, and visualizing happy outcomes. Relaxation and downtime will allow you to focus on your strengths. You are in control. You can navigate difficult times by working yourself up, or by calming yourself down. Go for the latter.

Be open to communication. Listen. Talk with people you respect, trust, and who can support you as you tackle challenges. Share ideas. Ask questions. Chat about procrastination. Use a steady tone of voice. Don't be afraid to seek help if you feel you need it.

A shift in mindset from *"I can't"* or *"I won't,"* to *"I can and I will!"* will help you to become more productive. Consider what really matters to you, and then how you will make time for those things.

But above all, stay calm. *"Be like a duck. Calm on the surface but always paddling like the dickens underneath."*[65] That quote captures the image of doing what it takes to go forward, unruffled and keen.

Bringing out the best

It's been said that difficult times often bring out the best in people.[66] Procrastination can be difficult, and so when working to overcome it, your "best" can make all the difference. Not just your best *effort*, but all you've got. What are your finest attributes? What can you draw upon? What makes you tick?

Do you thrive on encouragement? Competition? Challenge? Are you motivated by curiosity? Fear? Success? What circumstances or surroundings help you to flourish? What gives you swagger, self-confidence, or willfulness, the kind that can propel you to greater accomplishment? Who and what can help you get there?

Get to know your feelings, attitudes, and habits. The good, and the not-so-good but fixable. The better you know yourself, the sooner you can get down to the business of tapping your strengths, bolstering your weaknesses, and doing what you have to do.

Marilyn Price-Mitchell, in her book *Tomorrow's Change Makers* and on her website, writes about eight interconnected abilities that drive personal, academic, career, and life success. The eight abilities are: empathy; integrity; creativity; curiosity; resilience; self-awareness; sociability; and resourcefulness. By nurturing these attributes, teens grow up to become *"caring family members, innovative workers, ethical leaders, and engaged citizens."*[67]

Last words

"You have brains in your head. You have feet in your shoes.
You can steer yourself in any direction you choose.
You're on your own, and you know what you know.
And you are the guy who'll decide where to go."

~ Dr. Seuss

I've always loved that particular quote! I believe that no matter how old you are, it's important to steer yourself well. It's also important to have faith in your ability to do whatever you set your mind to do.

When it comes to procrastinating and busting your BUTS…, there are many considerations—as you've seen throughout these pages. There are different reasons for procrastination, and I've shared hundreds of ideas about what you can do to prevent and manage it. And, in this final chapter, I've emphasized the power of possibility (while also taking into account the "don'ts"), as well as suggesting how to increase your motivation, hone your time management skills, and tap your strengths.

You may recall from the introduction of this book that I said that the responsibility for overcoming procrastination lies with you. It still does—but now you have a better understanding of the issues, and a large number of practical strategies you can use.

What's the most important strategy? That will depend on what underlies your behavior, and how committed you are to dealing with it. However, a first step is essential.

Resolve to take that first small step, whatever it is. Then keep going forward, so that soon your procrastination will become a thing of the past.

Ironically, you will have put it off!

The End

(But…also a fresh beginning.)

References

Brain Power Enrichment. www.brainpower.ca

Covey, S. (2014). *The 7 habits of highly effective teens.* Simon & Schuster.

Doidge, N. (2007). *The brain that changes itself.* Penguin.

Duckworth, A. L. (2016). *Grit: The power of passion and perseverance.* Scribner.

Dweck, C. S. (2006). *Mindset: The new psychology of success.* Ballantine Books.

Ellis, A. & Harper, R. A. (1975). *A guide to rational living.* Wilshire Book Company.

Elyé, B. (2017). *Teen success! Ideas to move your mind.* Great Potential Press.

Foster, J. F. *Fostering Kids' Success,* column at The Creativity Post. www.creativitypost.com

Foster, J. F. (2015). *Not now, maybe later: Helping children overcome procrastination.* Great Potential Press.

Goertzel, V.; Goertzel, M. G., Goertzel T. G.; & Hansen, A. M. W. (2004). *Cradles of eminence: Childhoods of more than 700 famous men and women* (2nd ed.). Great Potential Press.

Goleman, D. (2005). *Emotional intelligence: Why it can matter more than IQ.* Bantam Books.

Greenspon, T. (2012). *Moving past perfect; How perfectionism may be holding back your kids (and you!) and what you can do about it.* Free Spirit Press.

Halsted, J. W. (2002). *Some of my best friends are books: Guiding gifted readers from preschool to high school. 3rd edition.* Great Potential Press.

Kaufman, S. B. Blog accessible at www.scottbarykaufman.com; Author of (2013) *Ungifted—Intelligence redefined; The truth about talent, practice, creativity, and the many paths to greatness.* Basic Books.

Kerr, B. & McKay, R. (2014). *Smart girls in the 21st century: Understanding talented girls and women.* Great Potential Press.

Kids Now Canada. www.kidsnowcanada.org/

Kruse, K. (2015). *15 secrets successful people know about time management.* The Kruse Group.

Lahey, J. (2016). *The gift of failure: How the best parents let go so their children can succeed.* Harper Collins.

LaPointe, V. Blog accessible at www.drvanessalapointe.com; Author of (2016) *Discipline without damage: How to get your kids to behave without messing them up.* Lifetree Media.

Lewis, C. S. (2004). *Chronicles of Narnia.* Harper Collins.

Matthews, D. J. & Foster, J. F. (2014). *Beyond intelligence: Secrets for raising happily productive kids.* House of Anansi Press.

Matthews, D. J. & Foster, J. F. (2009). *Being smart about gifted education: A guidebook for educators and parents.* Great Potential Press.

Neihart, M. (2008). *Peak performance for smart kids.* Prufrock Press.

Orlando, J. Blog accessible at www.joanneorlando.com

Peters, D. (2014). *From worrier to warrior: A guide to conquering your fears*. Great Potential Press.

Price-Mitchell, M. Blog accessible at www.rootsofaction.com; Author of (2015) *Tomorrow's change-makers: Reclaiming the power of citizenship for a new generation*. Eagle Harbor Publishing.

Procrastination Research Group, Carlton University. www.procrastination.ca

Radcliffe, S. C. (2014). *The fear fix: Solutions for every child's moments of worry, panic, and fear*. Harper Collins.

Reh, F. J. *Pareto's principle: The 80/20 rule* at www.thebalance.com/pareto-s-principle-the-80-20-rule-2275148

Reivich, K. & Shatté, A. (2003). *The resilience factor: 7 keys to finding your inner strength and overcoming life's hurdles*. Harmony.

Rowling, J. K. (1997). *Harry Potter and the philosopher's stone*. Bloomsbury.

Seligman, M. (2006). *Learned optimism: How to change your mind and your* life. Vintage.

Shanker, S. Blog accessible at www.self-reg.ca; Author of (2012) *Calm, alert, and learning: Classroom strategies for self-regulation*. Pearson, Canada.

Van Gemert, L. (2017). *Perfectionism: A practical guide to managing "never good enough."* Great Potential Press.

Vardy, M. (2013). *The productivityist workbook*. Amazon digital services.

Webb, J. T. (2013). *Searching for meaning: Idealism, bright minds, disillusionment, and hope*. Great Potential Press.

Webb, J. T., Gore, J. L., Amend, E.R., & DeVries, A. R. (2007). *A parent's guide to gifted children*. Great Potential Press.

Weinman, M. (2014). *It's about time: Transforming chaos into calm, A to Z.* iUniverse Inc.

Yousafzai, M. (2013). *I am Malala: How one girl stood up for education and changed the world.* Little, Brown, and Company.

Endnotes

1   An inability to make decisions goes hand in hand with procrastination. In Beatrice J. Elyé's book, *Teen Success! Ideas to Move Your Mind*, the author provides step-by-step suggestions for making wise decisions, including the best way (for you!) to approach seemingly massive tasks or problems. For example, on pages 51 through 56 of that book, she describes five steps: defining the problem, setting a goal, hypothesizing solutions, ranking judgment (which means determining which possible solutions make the most sense based on the situation and then ranking them), and making the decision. All helpful guidelines!

2   For interesting quotes, go to www.brainyquote.com and put a key word in the search engine. Enjoy!

3   If you want to use creativity to help you get going, these questions will provide a starting point: 1. What do you already know? (Knowledge is a basis for creative activity.) 2. How can you take what you know and use it effectively? (That is, thoughtfully, correctly.) 3. How can you take what you know and use it in fresh ways? (New approaches.) 4. How can you take what you know and use it to improve how you think about the situation? 5. What resources are available?

4   Dr. Vanessa LaPointe, a psychologist who lives and works in British Columbia, is the author of the book *Discipline without Damage*. She believes that boredom can be beneficial. She writes, *"Children need to sit in the nothingness of boredom in order to arrive at an understanding of who they are. And just as important, children need to sit in the nothingness of boredom to awaken their own internal drive to be."* This advice applies to teens and adults, too. www.drvanessalapointe.com posted on May 1, 2016.

5   Self-advocacy tips: When speaking up it's important to be fair-minded, and respectfully assertive. You can connect what you have to do with what you know, and with what else is happening in your life. Your behavior can contribute to your problems, but it can also contribute to your advancement and well-being. You have the power to use your interests and strengths as springboards to happiness and success. Hold onto your values, and stay motivated. Work alongside trusted adults or friends who can support your efforts.

6   On pages 141-143 of *Not Now, Maybe Later* I discuss the difference between doing something adequately, proficiently, or masterfully. I tell the story of Pauline who has to do an assignment about "24 hours in the life of..." She has to choose a setting—like a beach, a rock, or a field. She selects the park across the road from her house but she really has no interest in the project. She begins by thinking she will do an *adequate* job (bare basics). Then she becomes more interested in the dynamics of the park, and she aspires to be *proficient* (thoughtful and detailed). Finally, she acquires a *mastery orientation* as she engages fully with what's happening in the park by using all her senses, and by being effortful, creative, and extremely thorough.

7   Here's a link to a site that provides an in-depth list of interesting fictional characters and their various superpowers. You aren't on the list (for better or worse), but...you *can* call upon your strengths, and even develop new ones, that will give you a purposeful and energized boost, and enhance your will and your ability to do things—*now.* https://en.wikipedia.org/wiki/List_of_superhuman_features_and_abilities_in_fiction)

8   It's important to develop a growth mindset. Don't be afraid to talk about challenge and frustration. Try to master difficult tasks by being more persistent and resilient. There's a learning curve involved, so developing a growth mindset is not always easy—but it's worth the effort. It will help you see things through when the going gets tough. Plus, conquering tricky or hard situations will make you feel more confident. We grow by doing, and by pushing ourselves to deal with setbacks that arise.

9   Check out this article. It's on believing in yourself. www.rootsofaction.com -manifesto-youth/ Key words that appear within the article include *learn, aware, values, goals, inspired,* and *meaningful.*

10 There are various word cloud sites but the one I used here is www.wordclouds.com

11   Two books that are designed to help children and teens deal with fears are *The Fear Fix: Solutions for Every Child's Moments of Worry, Panic, and Fear,* by Sarah Chana Radcliffe www.sarahchanaradcliffe.com/the-fear-fix/ and *From Worrier to Warrior: A Guide to Conquering Your Fears,* by Dan Peters www.drdanpeters.com. And, although it's a bit sophisticated, here's an interesting article by Henry L. Roediger, from *Scientific American:* www.scientificamerican.com/article/getting-it-wrong/

12   See *The Brain that Changes Itself,* by Norman Doidge, for information about how people can actually create new patterns of feeling and thinking through neuroplasticity—the brain's ability to rewire neural pathways.

13   *The Fear Fix,* by Sarah Chana Radcliffe, p. 297.

14   For more on overcoming challenges while doing or creating, here is a link to an article I co-created with artist Rina Gottesman, published at *The Creativity Post:* www.creativitypost.com/education/challenges_of_creativity

15   The melting clock that appears on the back cover of my book *Not Now, Maybe Later,* and again on *Bust Your BUTS* is a famous image created by artist Salvador Dali. The original oil on canvas painting, on exhibit at the Metropolitan Museum of Modern Art in New York, features several of these clocks—and time appears to be melting away. Interestingly, the title of Dali's painting is "The Persistence of Memory." To find out more about this intriguing work of art, go to www.moma.org/learn/moma_learning/1168-2. It might be worth noting that persistence relates to more than just memory. It also affects achievement, work ethic, risk-taking, and confidence building.

16   *The Gift of Failure,* by Jessica Lahey www.jessicalahey.com/the-gift-of-failure/ In this book, the author puts an alternative spin on failure and struggle. She sees them as valuable learning opportunities—hence the word "gift" in the title. Lahey also discusses the development of competence, independence, and identity formation (getting to know yourself), and how to strengthen these capacities. She explains that *"setbacks, mistakes, miscalculations, and failures"* are experiences that teach kids how to be *"resourceful, persistent, innovative and resilient citizens of this world."* (p. xii) This book is written for parents (including those who *"overparent"*), but the message—having to do with kids striving toward accomplishments

even when they encounter "*uncomfortable bumps and obstacles*"—is one that teens can appreciate, too.

17   The book *Cradles of Eminence: Childhoods of More than 700 Famous Men and Women* is an inspiring read. You will discover how people from different cultures and various walks of life overcame difficulties, and ultimately became accomplished in their respective fields.

18   In *Being Smart about Gifted Education: A Guidebook for Educators and Parents*, Dona Matthews and I discuss healthy development, including why it's important to commit to your "authentic self," and not to "cave in" for purposes of social pressure or other reasons. Dumbing-down tends to be more prevalent among girls (see *Smart Girls in the 21st Century: Understanding Talented Girls and Women*, by Barbara Kerr and Robin McKay), but many boys also engage in this kind of behavior or thinking. Parents and teachers can help teens recharge, stay true to themselves and their levels of competence, and strategically build upon that. We offer many suggestions for this throughout the book, however we focus exclusively on adolescent issues on pages 210-220.

19   It's often easier to label and understand happy, positive feelings than it is to understand those that are upsetting. It might be helpful to start by just focusing on naming the upsetting feeling, rather than trying to fix it right away. Once you know what it is (for example, feeling hurt, or frustrated), then you can start to figure out why it's happened and what to do about it.

20   Children and teens from two First Nations communities near Saskatoon, Canada attend Cando Community School where teacher Janice Reade and her colleagues have adopted a system to help teens with self-regulation. In Grades 10, 11, and 12, they use a five-point scale—one is hyper, five is not alert, and three is just right. From kindergarten through Grade nine, children use a three-point scale—Tigger (hyper), Eyore (not alert), and Pooh (just right). When teens have trouble dealing with their emotions, they've learned to use different strategies such as physical activity, playing with fidget toys, or engaging in slow, deep breathing to get themselves back to "just right."

21   Psychologist Daniel Goleman has written many books and articles on emotional intelligence. You can check out his materials online, including an audio book geared to helping teens focus by enhancing concentration, and staying calm. Also, a great article

on self-regulation for teens, written by Sara Westbrook, can be found at www.linkedin.com/pulse/how-self-regulation-empowers-young-people-move-beyond-sara. Finally, Stuart Shanker's work on self-regulation is worth a look. Go to www.self-reg.ca

22 The book *Perfectionism: A Practical Guide to Managing "Never Good Enough"* offers strategies for understanding and dealing with perfectionism. Author Lisa Van Gemert discusses causes and pays attention to both the upsides and the downsides (including negative thinking, stress, and lack of motivation), as well as key issues like goals, habits, and the pursuit of excellence. She discusses the importance of building self-confidence and resilience, and offers tips to help teens live in the moment and to accept imperfection. The book is full of practical strategies for those seeking to cope with—and curb—perfectionism tendencies.

23 Canadian-based sites that offer assistance with bullying and teasing incidents include www.kidshelpphone.ca www.stopbullying.gov stopbullyingcanada.wordpress.com Schools and local police stations also offer helpful resources. (See endnote 52 as well.)

24 From the movie *Kungfu Panda 3*. It's a popular animated feature, and the quote packs a punch.

25 In Lisa Van Gemert's book, *Perfectionism: A Practical Guide to Managing "Never Good Enough,"* you will find out why failure is valuable, and discover the power of a ninety-nine—along with many other helpful tips. For example, she writes," *If you get a one hundred right away, you will have nowhere to grow. What we want is not to try for a hundred, but to try for growth.*" p. 100.

26 From *Moving Past Perfect; How Perfectionism May be Holding Back Your Kids (And You!) And What You Can Do About It.* Thomas S. Greenspon, Free Spirit Publishing, p. xl.

27 In the book *Searching for Meaning: Idealism, Bright Minds, Disillusionment, and Hope*, author James T. Webb discusses how to manage emotional states, including how to change disillusionment into opportunities for growth. Dr. Webb describes many of life's difficulties and concerns, and he provides guidelines for developing awareness, acknowledgment, appreciation, and acceptance of oneself. In *Searching for Meaning,* readers will learn valuable coping styles to help them overcome depression, balance day-to-day challenges, and attain contentment.

28   Dr. James T. Webb is a psychologist who has written a great deal about depression. I am grateful to him for sharing his expertise here: *"Depression in teens is often shrugged off by adults as developmentally normal—just a stage, or because of "bad influence" of peers, lack of sleep, or even poor eating habits. But depression is real. It is a mood state that lasts at least two weeks, during which the person has a general loss of interest or pleasure, and usually withdraws from others and has less energy. Sometimes, too, the person's appetite and sleep patterns change, and there may be difficulty thinking and concentrating.*

Most people think that depression is shown in low self-esteem, sadness, weepiness, hopelessness, self-blame, helplessness, and general despondency. Certainly, that is true for many people, but it is important to know that many children and adolescents who are depressed show a mood that is more irritable than sad, with rudeness, temper outbursts, or poor school performance. In others, the depression is expressed through boredom, restlessness, vague illnesses, or daydreaming. Depressed girls are more likely to withdraw; boys are particularly prone to antisocial negative behaviors such as aggression, rudeness, restlessness, sulking, various school problems, and drug or alcohol abuse. Some depressed adolescents feel so disappointed in themselves and the world that they will cut their arms or legs to punish themselves or because the pain is the only thing that reminds them that they are still alive; others try to escape with drugs and alcohol.

Whatever the surface behaviors, most depressed individuals feel hurt and angry inside, but they also feel helpless to do anything about it. Though unhappy with their current life situation, they feel powerless to make the necessary changes. They generally focus on themselves, feel hopeless, and seem unable to muster enough energy to even attempt helpful problem solving. This, of course, can lead to significant procrastination. If you feel depressed, please realize that you do not have to continue to be that way. You can seek a counselor or talk with a trusted adult or health care professional."

29   To find out more about circadian rhythm, go to sleepfoundation. org/sleep-topics/what-circadian-rhythm.

30   Reference to a quote by Martin Luther King who said, *"You don't have to see the whole staircase, just take the first step."*

31   Here's an interesting article on self-talk. Http://au.reachout.com/ what-is-self-talk.

32 C. S. Lewis wrote the acclaimed *Chronicles of Narnia* fantasy books (which have sold over 100 million copies in 47 languages). Writing a series of books is an impressive goal and a remarkable accomplishment!

33 Psychologist and author Maureen Neihart talks about SMART goal-setting in her book *Peak Performance.*

34 "*People progress and have a greater chance of succeeding when they see setbacks as opportunities, and when they show resilience instead of giving up. Challenge can be fruitful. Overcoming obstacles can be motivating!*" Extracted from my article at *The Creativity Post*— "3 Ways to Support Kids' Intelligence and Creativity: What to Strive for When Life's a Whirlwind" www.creativitypost.com/education/

35 This reinforces the comment by Dale Carnegie that appears in the section of this book "BUT…I might do badly (fear of failure)." By the way, there are also some rather interesting worst case scenario survival handbooks you can read, with suggestions for preparing for and minimizing tricky or tough situations. (Such as warding off a bear attack, surviving when lost in the desert, or escaping from a sinking car, all of which actually might make dealing with your fears or difficulties—or procrastination—seem much less discouraging by comparison!)

36 In her book *It's about Time: Transforming Chaos into Calm, A to Z*, author Mitzi Weinman discusses ways to maximize productivity and time. www.timefinder.net She provides ideas and practical tools, many of which work for teens, too. For example, she talks about practices such as breaking down tasks, determining objectives, becoming committed, jump-starting your day, making and using to-do lists, sharing burdens, and, perhaps most importantly, setting aside and enjoying quality time—that is, time spent meaningfully on your own or with others.

37 I chose the title of my book "*Not Now, Maybe Later*" very deliberately. Although procrastination can certainly be—or become—problematic, there are times when *later* makes good sense, and *now* is just not feasible. People understand that—after all, they, too, have reasons for declining to do things sometimes—and so if you are courteous, and your justification for saying "*no thanks*" is reasonable, then they may be quite accepting of your stance.

38   In a column at *The Creativity Post*, I discuss the connections between prior knowledge and learning. This is an example I give: *Perhaps you want to write a story about someone caught in an avalanche or a tsunami. It would be difficult to do that without some knowledge of where and why avalanches or tsunamis occur, and what kinds of experiences people have had in such harrowing circumstances. Because you can't actually be "in" a natural disaster like this, you have to research the topic. You have to attain knowledge that then becomes a basis for learning, engagement, and creative activity. In the absence of this knowledge, there is little to grasp or go on. In every field of endeavor—mathematics, science, athleticism, the arts, you name it—growth and learning are predicated upon what's already known."* It's helpful to find out what else you need to know in order to extend your ideas thoughtfully and creatively. www.creativitypost.com/education/what_is_the_connection_between_prior_knowledge_and_learning1

39   Timeful, Evernote, and Focus Booster are the top productivity apps listed at this site, which offers suggestions for tech-based time management alternatives for students: www.topuniversities.com/blog/top-time-management-apps-students-2015 There are also "to-do" apps, and other useful apps listed as well. Take care, though, not to waste too much time shopping your way through scads of time-saving applications. That could defy the purpose.

40   From William Shakespeare's *Hamlet*, Act 2, Scene 2

41   Here's a link to an article about inspirational quotes, and how the experiences and words of others have the potential to propel you forward. www.creativitypost.com/education/through_the_lives_of_others_inspiring_childrens_creativity_and_productivity

42   For a humorous look at how distractions can jeopardize your best intentions, see the entertaining video clip *Procrastination—The Musical*, on You Tube.

43   This is called conditioning. And you don't have to use food. You could try dimes, checkmarks, or anything else that is reinforcing for you. Another approach would be to reward yourself every time a certain time period has elapsed (say 20 minutes). If you have not been distracted, or you have not procrastinated, you get the item/treat.

44   For more on mindfulness, you can refer to *Beyond Intelligence: Secrets for Raising Happily Productive Kids* (p. 233-237), and *Not*

Now, Maybe Later (p. 101), and check out the information at www. discovermindfulness.ca

45   Productivity author and consultant, Mike Vardy, talks about how *"frameworks foster freedom."* He has lots of good ideas on his website. See www.productivityist.com

46   This quote is extracted from an article at www.creativitypost.com/ education/challenges_of_creativity

47   I talk about power struggles in the first chapter of this book.

48   Be wary of counting on luck in order to get things done efficiently or effectively. You'll be able to make the most of opportunity by being prepared and able to manage your time. Luck is not reliable.

49   Written by Scott Barry Kaufman on April 23, 2016. Here is the rest of that post: *"I am certainly not gifted in everything, but I do admit at having an astonishing capacity to live up to people's expectations. When I am around someone who I feel thinks very little of me, I tend to act little, confirming their expectations. But when I am around someone who clearly expects something good to come out of me, goodness outpours from the depths of my soul, excitedly and enthusiastically. Clearly, this stems in large part from my early life experiences. But I'm just reflecting that the healthiest way of being is to not make one's inner outpouring of goodness dependent on anyone else's expectations or values. It needs to be a stable anchor deep within, that is uncontaminated by the prejudice and actions of others. Finding this anchor at all times has been one of the most difficult things for me to do in my adult life, but I have made a goal to increase its signal, and reduce the noise. Hopefully one day I can be myself—the good and the bad, the joy and the sorrow, the prosocial spirit, and the goofy naughtiness—on my own watch, under my own lock and key. I wish the same for all of you."*

50   See Seligman (2006) and Reivich & Shatté (2002) for more extensive descriptions of this kind of thinking and about the ABCDE model.

51   Ellis and Harper (1975), in their rational emotive behavior therapy, point out that almost all of our stress comes from our own irrational thinking, and they describe ways that we can challenge it. For example, if you start each day believing that you should do perfectly in all respects, you are setting yourself up for failure. It's an irrational thought, yet we sometimes find ourselves thinking that way.

52   Bullying is a relationship problem, and teasing can escalate and become hurtful and abusive. It helps to learn about conflict

resolution, and to develop coping mechanisms in advance. Four useful practices to manage your feelings and prevent bullying are: 1. Carefully think through the issues and alternative responses to others' comments and behavior before reacting. 2. Be tolerant, and think positively rather than suspiciously about what others say or do. Ask yourself, "*What's the best possible way to view the other person's words or actions?*" 3. Question inferences, learning to separate your perceptions of the issues from the actual facts of the situation. 4. Become aware of the possible consequences of your own actions. (Extracted from *Beyond Intelligence: Secrets for Raising Happily Productive Kids*, p. 217.) Schools have anti-bullying practices and policies in place. And, for assistance with bullying, cyber bullying, or victimhood, check out your local 24-hour kids help phone line. You can also find excellent information and resources online, including at nobullying.com/bullying-help-usa/ and at www.stompoutbullying.org

53   Dr. Joanne Orlando is a technology expert who studies the ways and extent to which people are "plugged in" to devices, and the multiple effects of that on learning, relationships, health, and other aspects of our lives. If you go to Dr. Orlando's website you'll find many relevant articles on family technology use and screen time, and tips for functioning more effectively in what has become a "*digitally distracting world*." www.joanneorlando.com

54   Angela Duckworth, who has conducted many research studies, has written a book titled *Grit: The Power of Passion and Perseverance*. angeladuckworth.com She notes that you can make your study environment more effective by hiding your smartphone and turning off the Internet modem. Then you won't be tempted or distracted.

55   Google "hero's journey examples in books" to see a range of diagrams.

56   Here is how the 12 step Hero's Journey plays out in the story of *Cinderella*: 1. ordinary world—Cinderella's family dynamic; 2. call to adventure—the ball at the palace; 3. refusal of the call—Cinderella is not able to go; 4. meeting the mentor—the fairy godmother; 5. crossing the threshold—Cinderella will be able to go to the ball: 6. test, allies, enemies—the pumpkin carriage, the dress, the glass slippers; 7. approach—Cinderella dances with the prince; 8. the central ordeal—Cinderella falls in love; 9. the reward—the prince has fallen in love; 10. the road back—midnight and Cinderella returns to her old life; 11. resurrection—the glass slipper fits; 12. return with the elixir—the prince and Cinderella marry, and they live happily ever after.

57   Quote attributed to Eleanor Roosevelt, U.S. First Lady, diplomat, and activist.

58   www.scribd.com/document/195749719/101-Great-Books-Recommended-for-College-Bound-Readers.

59   TIME's list of top 100 books for children and also for teens: time.com/100-best-childrens-books/ and time.com/100-best-young-adult-books/

60   In the Toronto area, where I live, there are more programs than I could possibly list here, in all kinds of areas including math, chess, robotics, kitchen chemistry, astronomy, and on and on…Two interesting options include the *Kids Now* program for middle school students, with a focus on making positive choices, resilience, self-confidence, leadership, teamwork, and more—www.kidsnowcanada.org, and the *Brain Power Enrichment* programs, with a focus on critical thinking skills, knowledge exploration, problem solving, and other wonderful brain-building experiences for kids in Grades 2 through 12—www.brainpower.ca

61   For more on Sean Covey's work, visit www.seancovey.com. His book geared for teens is a bestseller. (FYI—The seven habits he discusses at length are: be proactive; begin with the end in mind; put first things first; think win-win; seek first to understand, then to be understood; synergize; and sharpen the saw. You can learn about each of these habits by reading the book!)

62   An Internet search will provide much more additional information on Kevin Kruse and time management.

63   This principle has an economic origin. It's attributed to economist Vilfreto Pareto, who states that 80% of benefits derive from 20% of investments. Or, in other words, 80% of results are the result of only 20% of the causes. This principle applies to various aspects of life including, for example, work habits, relationships, and nutrition. How much time do we actually waste on non-productive effort? Also, here's an interesting article by F. John Reh, illustrating the Pareto Principle. www.thebalance.com/pareto-s-principle-the-80-20rule-2275148.

64   Check out *Timefinder* by Mitzi Weinman: www.timefinder.net/blog/?category=Parents

65   Quote accredited to actor Michael Caine.

66 This view has been attributed to U S. presidential candidate Bernie Sanders, although I suspect many others have expressed the same sentiment over the years.

67 For more information on Marilyn Price-Mitchell's compass advantage model, visit her website at: www.rootsofaction.com

About the Author

Joanne Foster has a Master's degree in Special Education and Adaptive Instruction, and a Doctoral degree in Human Development and Applied Psychology from the University of Toronto. She is a parent, teacher, gifted education specialist, university instructor, educational consultant, and award-winning author who has worked in the field of gifted education for over 30 years. She conducts teacher-training workshops, gives presentations to educators and parent organizations in local, national, and international forums, and serves on several advisory committees concerning children's education and optimal development. She is co-author (with Dona Matthews) of *Being Smart about Gifted Education* (2009), and *Beyond Intelligence: Secrets for Raising Happily Productive Kids* (2014). Dr. Foster is also the sole author of *Not Now, Maybe Later: Helping Children Overcome Procrastination* (2015). She wrote "ABCs of Being Smart," a series of feature articles for the National Association for Gifted Children's magazine *Parenting for High Potential*, and her column "Fostering Kids' Success" appears at *The Creativity Post* online. Her writing appears in many other publications around the world. Dr. Foster has taught Educational Psychology at the Ontario Institute for Studies in Education of the University of Toronto for twelve years, and she continues to provide leadership across the broader community in the areas of giftedness and high-level development.

www.joannefoster.ca
www.beyondintelligence.net

Lightning Source UK Ltd.
Milton Keynes UK
UKOW06f2014131017
310925UK00024B/1776/P